A Nurse's
ANTIDOTE

THE WILL OF GOD IS THE CURE

Connie Cleaver

Chapter 1: Introduction Unveiling my Journey

Introducing the Author - A Glimpse into My Life and Struggles

"I have said these things to you, that in me you may have peace. In the world you will have tribulation. But take heart; I have overcome the world."

John 16:33

You can travel through the kaleidoscope of my past by putting yourself in my position and feeling the gentle pull of my memories and feelings. Step into my shoes. You come of age in a quiet town tucked away in the heart of a tight-knit society whose values are more than just empty platitudes. But, as is the case with many stories, things are not quite as calm as they appear to be at first glance. You go through difficult experiences that mold the young girl you are on the inside, creating vivid strokes of uncertainty on the canvas that is your mind.

The communities you pass through and the schools you go to are all silent witnesses to the decisions you've made in an attempt to find legitimacy in your life. Your stories, as someone who was merely searching for affirmation in places and people who could only offer fleeting relief, are carried by the winds as they whisper.

And yet, despite all of this commotion, a calm force is continually pulling at your heart, and that force is your steadfast faith. This faith serves as an anchor for you, protecting you from being carried away by the waves of life no matter how turbulent the seas of life may become. The teachings of Christianity are not simply a collection of verses to be memorized; rather, they are the very lifelines that one clings to when they are surrounded by uncertainty.

As one moves through the stages of early adulthood, the web of interpersonal connections grows more complex. But there is one relationship in particular, with a man named John, that puts the very core of your sense of value to the test. When you're around him, the dance of being "an option" turns into an all-too-familiar waltz, with each step mirroring the desire to be prioritized more than the previous one.

Even under these nuanced circumstances, there is a realization that can be incredibly unsettling: if you are dating a married man, what do you really have? The answer, even though it hurts, is very obvious. A simple text message can be the spark that breaks the illusion and compels you to face what you see when you look in the mirror. The woman who is staring back at you longs for much more than fleeting moments of intimacy; she wants a love that is unquestionably hers.

And now, you find yourself engaged in a quest, not merely for the sake of affection or affirmation, but also to find a sense of wholeness that cannot be discovered in the shadow of another. Your faith serves as a constant reminder to you that the love of God is the one and only genuine love, a compass that will never fail to lead you back to safety.

When I was a young girl, my entire universe consisted of our humble home, which was situated in a quiet neighborhood of a small town. My name is Connie, and within the confines of that house and the limits of that town, I was able to experience the entire gamut of human emotion, from the most unadulterated happiness to the most heartbreaking grief.

The maze that is childhood is not always an easy one to navigate. Many people describe it as being full of the joy of sharing new experiences, the merriment of spending time with family, and the excitement of making new friends. But for me, it frequently seemed more like a labyrinth than a maze. The hallways were littered with traces of uncertainty, nooks filled with isolation, and dead ends that seared with excruciating pain. I had no idea where I was going and was always looking for a way out or a glimpse of hope.

For me, school was more like an unforgiving battlefield, even though it was supposed to be a safe haven where I could study and explore new things. Whereas other children flourished, I frequently had the sensation that I was withering away, my petals being peeled away one at a time by the vicious winds of derision and rejection. My nights were frequently spent with quiet sobs as the weight of the day's events pressed down on me, crushing my developing sense of self-worth and leaving me feeling smaller and more unimportant than I had previously felt.

But even at those times of hopelessness, when it felt as though the walls were closing in, there was always a gentle light that beckoned. That ray of light represented my confidence. My relationship with God was the thread that weaved through the fabric of my life, transforming it from a drab grey to a vivid rainbow in the process. Every Bible verse I read was like a lifeline, and every prayer I said was like a conversation.

When I was feeling abandoned by the world, I would take consolation in the pages of the Bible and let the stories of hope, love, and redemption wrap around me like a warm blanket. Those stories helped me feel like I wasn't alone in the world. The teachings of God became my armor, protecting me from the arrows of skepticism and contempt that were frequently shot in my direction. I was able to assimilate the teachings of love and compassion as I read through each text. I realized that I am a wonderful child, deserving of love and destined for greatness in God's sight, and I learned to see myself in this light.

Even though they broke my heart at the time, the challenges I faced in my youth helped pave the way for my journey of self-discovery. Every cut, every scrape, every tear was a learning experience that helped shape me, refine me, and get me ready for the upcoming struggles and victories that lie ahead. My faith was tested to its limits during these difficult times in my upbringing, but it emerged stronger than ever. It turned out to be the cornerstone upon which I constructed the rest of my life, a life that, in spite of the difficulties it presented in the beginning, eventually flowered into one that was filled with undying love, purpose, and trust.

Revisiting those years in my mind, I perceive not only the pain but also the divine splendor that resided within the journey. When observed through the divine lens of my spirituality, I perceive that the trials I have triumphed over have not been imposed upon me as retributions but rather as sacred invitations for me to gain wisdom and evolve as a soul, enabling me to embrace an existence that is enriched and gratifying. It is a life in which my spirituality transcends being a mere fragment of my being but rather becomes the essence that shapes my very identity.

You may have always thought that when someone cares for you, they will look out for your best interests. When I was a kid, I always had the impression that love meant protecting someone from harm and making sure they were insulated from the more difficult aspects of

life. But as the years passed, the waters became murkier, and you gradually came to the conclusion that not all claims of protection were genuine. Sometimes, a face of control, manipulation, and maltreatment lay beneath the mask of compassion that was worn all the time.

When you first stepped foot into the realm of romantic partnerships, you were a blank canvas, ready to be painted with a masterpiece that embodied love, trust, and mutual respect. However, even though the first blows appeared to be mild, they were anything but. He would tell her things like, "Don't wear that outfit; it's too revealing," or "Why do you need to go out with those people? Continue to accompany me. On the surface, the comments looked to express anxiety; nevertheless, upon closer inspection, they revealed the first signs of an approaching storm.

It started out as a mere concern. There was a never-ending stream of calls and messages. "Just checking in," he would explain, or "I worry about you when I don't hear from you." You got the impression that this care wasn't genuine despite the fact that, on the surface, it appeared to be kind. It was control masked as caring attention in order to fool others.

Soon enough, the lines became less distinct. Every single

choice and decision was put under the microscope. The globe, which had previously appeared huge and infinite, gave the impression of contracting into a cage. Friends took notice of the shift and inquired in a concerned manner as to whether or not everything was all right. But how could you possibly justify something that was so sneaky? To the outside world, he appeared to be a devoted and concerned lover who would do anything to protect his girlfriend. But you should have known better. Underneath that superficial display of concern was a wish to control, manipulate, and dominate the situation.

The damage done to your mental state was obvious to everyone. Your sense of self-worth was diminished with each and every remark and "suggestions" offered. You started to become a shadow of the once vibrant person you used to be, someone who was always questioning their decisions and anxious all the time. You used to be full of hopes and aspirations.

But even in the midst of the chaos, a clear picture started to emerge. You saw through the deception and saw that it was not love but rather control; that it was not protection but rather possession. The difference between genuine compassion and control gained through manipulation was brought into sharper focus. Authentic love energizes, uplifts, and fosters personal development. On the other side, control is detrimental to one's spirit because it stifles, suppresses, and dampens it.

You started over piece by piece, recovering your identity, resetting the bounds of your life, and reasserting the value you provide to the world. The trek was not simple, but with each footfall, a burden was removed, and the world became brighter.

When everything first began, the world had the appearance of being colored in the brightest shades of pink. The loving and cautious prods of concern, as well as the careful observations of my behaviors, seemed to be wrapped in a cloak of warmth and attention at all times. But as the days turned into nights and the seasons changed, I started to see the paint peeling off, revealing a disturbing undercoat. This unpleasant undercoat was a sign that something was wrong.

Every decision that I made was scrutinized to an excruciating degree. Everything I did, from the books I read to the people I kept in my life, was subject to close examination. Why are you spending your time reading that? There is better literature out there," or "Why waste time with them when there is greater literature out there?" They do not have the same level of concern for you that I do. Even though they were couched in terms of care, these remarks carried an underlying tone of superiority and a hint of control.

There is one particular occurrence that will never leave my memory. It was just a trip to the grocery shop, nothing special or out of the ordinary at all. However, even this was discussed in detail during the debriefing session. "Why did you purchase this particular brand? You must be unaware that the other option is superior, right? I assumed you'd be more aware than that." It was an aha! moment at that very time. The words, which appeared to be made out of kindness, were, in reality, attempts to manipulate my decision-making process.

The loneliness was by far the most difficult aspect. Friends, who were once my support system, are now only a distant memory. Every plan was viewed with a healthy dose of suspicion. "Is it absolutely necessary for you to see them once more? Have you not invested enough time in getting to know them?" I was aware of the irony that existed. The same individual who told me they were looking out for my best interests was the very same person who was blocking off my escape routes.

The oppressive awareness that one was being watched and evaluated started to take its toll. My normally exuberant attitude appeared to have become restrained. My anxiety started following me around all the time, and it would constantly plant seeds of doubt in my mind. "Perhaps they do have a point. It's possible that I don't know what would be best for me." It looked as though the walls were closing in on us, and the outside world started to look terrifying.

But when I was sitting there in the suffocating silence of my chamber each night, a soft voice would whisper to me and remind me of who I was before all of this. The young lady, who had an infectious giggle, was known to dance in the rain and loved with her whole heart. She remained there, waiting and hoping for anything to happen.

It wasn't an easy challenge for me to find my way back to her. It involved facing up to uncomfortable truths, admitting that one was being manipulated, and seeking assistance. Friends who, despite being alienated from me, gathered around me and were my anchors. Healing spaces emerged, and the mist began to lift in a methodical and steady fashion.

Even though they may be fraught with suffering, doubt, and uncertainty, the transforming moments that occur throughout life have a beauty to them. During times like this, we are frequently faced with decisions that will have a significant impact on the course our lives will take.

After I had my personal revelations, the world presented itself to me as a maze to navigate. Every avenue was a choice, and each one led to a different possible outcome. The well-trodden, familiar roads beckoned, bringing the promise of security to the traveler. However, woven throughout were lesser-traveled routes, ones that held the promise of development but came at the expense of a degree of suffering.

It is never simple to move away from what you are familiar with. Countless times, I was kept awake by the fear that coming into the unknown would result in my tripping and falling.

Despite this, there was an undercurrent of exhilaration running underneath the worry. This presented me with the opportunity to rewrite my story and stake a claim in a narrative in which I play the leading role rather than a supporting one.

Leaving one's comfort zone doesn't involve making a single, decisive leap; rather, it involves making a series of tiny, consistent steps. It is about choosing a path of resistance, even when the world around you presents you with easy opportunities to give in to temptation. Every time I took a step, my old anxieties—fears of inadequacy and failure, respectively—tried to pull me back. But a fresh burst of self-assurance would emerge after successfully overcoming each obstacle.

Chapter 2: Childhood Struggles and Mistreatment in Disguise

The Illusion of Protective Attention — Overcoming Adversity

"Dear friends, do not be surprised at the fiery ordeal that has come on you to test you, as though something strange were happening to you. "

Peter 4:12

I was born as the fourth of six children to a single mother, and our life was defined by struggles that seemed never-ending. While we may not have had the togetherness that some families enjoyed, there was a peculiar kind of unity in our shared adversity. We all knew what it meant to face hardships, and we faced them together in our own way.

One of the most challenging aspects of my childhood was the bullying I endured at school. It felt like I was an easy target, maybe because I wore my vulnerability on my sleeve. I vividly recall a particular incident that left an indelible mark on my young psyche. A classmate had offered me some clothes, which, given our impoverished situation, I gratefully accepted. The next day, I wore one of the shirts she had given me. Little did I know that this would become a moment etched in my memory forever.

As I entered the classroom, she couldn't contain her disdain. In front of the entire class, she pointed at me and said, "I knew you were gonna wear that shirt." The room erupted in laughter at my expense, and I felt like the walls were closing in on me. But the worst was yet to come. She sat down behind me, her intentions far from innocent. With a pair of scissors, she reached up and cut my earlobe, causing it to bleed onto the shirt. She sneered and said, "Maybe you'll wash it now."

The humiliation, pain, and shock of that moment were overwhelming. It was a horrifying experience that I could never forget. But it was also a pivotal moment that shaped the person I would become. In that instant, I made a silent vow to myself—I would never let anyone see me cry again. I couldn't bear the thought of being the object of ridicule, and I was determined to shield myself from further emotional wounds.

That incident marked the beginning of my journey. I learned to build a protective armor around my emotions, creating a facade that hid my vulnerability. It wasn't easy, but over time, I grew stronger. My self-esteem, once fragile, began to rebuild itself brick by brick. I realized that I couldn't control the cruelty of others, but I could control my response to it.

The teachers were supposed to be more than just educators; they were meant to be mentors, confidants, and guiding lights. However, the reality I faced was often far from this ideal. I understood that as a child, I bore no blame for the circumstances I was born into, and yet, the educators in my life played a role in shaping my perception of the world.

There were instances when teachers seemed to have their own judgments about our family's struggles. For example, if a child couldn't contribute to class parties, they were ostracized and made to sit in the hallway, excluded from the simple joys that others took for granted. This isolation further emphasized the disparities in our lives and created a sense of otherness.

There was another incident where a teacher marked my back. It was meant to be a sign that I hadn't bathed at home, a cruel commentary on my family's circumstances. I may have been young, but I wasn't naive. I knew what was expected, and I wasn't about to let anyone define me by their standards. With determination, I made my way to the water fountain and wiped away the mark. What did they take me for? I may have been a child, but I had my pride.

These experiences at the hands of teachers were not only hurtful but also demonstrated a lack of empathy for the challenges my family faced. Our single mother, struggling to provide for six children on meager welfare assistance, was doing her best with the limited opportunities available to her. Our meager monthly allowance of $243 painted a bleak picture of our financial circumstances. Survival was a constant battle, and the odds were stacked against us.

Yet, instead of understanding and compassion, some teachers chose to sit in judgment, discussing the shortcomings of my mother, who was simply trying to make ends meet. It was a harsh reality check for a child to witness the adults around them passing judgment on a situation they had no control over.

The memories of those early childhood experiences still linger in my mind, casting a long shadow over my adult life. Being excluded from class parties while everyone else celebrated left me with deep emotional scars. Even today, I find it difficult to join in on celebrations and gatherings. It's as though that sense of not belonging has become an intrinsic part of who I am.

I carry with me a sense of distrust and caution when it comes to forming friendships and connections with people. The wounds of those formative years run deep, and they've made me hesitant to let others in. It's not that I don't want to celebrate or be a part of social events, but the fear of rejection and exclusion often holds me back.

One thing that did provide solace during those trying times was the unity of my family. After school, when we returned home, my mother would gather us together, and we would sing gospel songs. Her beautiful voice would fill the room, and for those moments, we could forget about what we lacked and focus on lifting our spirits through song. It was a way for us to find comfort and strength in our shared faith, a faith that was a constant presence in our lives.

Although I wasn't taken to church regularly, as I was one of the younger children, my mother's singing and her connection to her older children who attended church created a sense of separation that I carried with me. It was a feeling of being left behind, not just physically but emotionally as well. The unspoken abandonment I felt was something I never expressed to her, as I knew she was doing her best to provide for our family. She faced incredible challenges as a single mother trying to support six children, and she did everything in her power to provide for us. Her strength was a source of inspiration for me, even if I grappled with the feelings of being left behind.

The bullying, poverty, and constant neediness were the foundational challenges that shaped my journey toward adulthood. These struggles were like a heavy cloud that hung over my early years, and they tested me in countless ways.

Another memory that will perhaps linger in my mind forever is the day we were walking to school, strolling along the sidewalk, when one of the girls suddenly spat on me. The act itself was degrading and humiliating. She was bigger than me, and I felt powerless to respond. The fear held me back from confronting her. Instead, I quietly made my way to the water fountain, washed my face, and continued on to class. What else could I do?

The feeling of not being enough, of never having enough, and the constant mockery weighed heavily on my young shoulders. What I once considered cool had become unbearable. School, which should have been a place of learning and growth, became a source of dread. It was a catch-22—either you didn't have enough, or you faced the torment of bullies.

The small solace of breakfast and lunch provided some comfort, but the challenges we encountered with our peers were traumatizing. Every day felt like a battle, navigating through a minefield of potential tormentors.

Soon enough, I had a realization that would change the course of my academic journey. I understood that if I could excel in the smart classes, I wouldn't have to endure the same hardships in the average classes, as most of the bullies weren't particularly academically inclined. So, I made it a goal to stay in those accelerated classes, and I succeeded. It became a habit to strive for excellence. I discovered that I was smart and capable of understanding and excelling in my studies. I took pride in my ability to complete my homework before returning home, and I cherished the good grades that came with it.

Growing up without both parents and lacking the necessary supplies and resources left me feeling like I was perpetually "less than." I internalized the perceptions of others and began to see myself through their eyes. My self-esteem suffered, initially making me believe the negative labels that were unfairly attached to me. "Dirty" and "not having anything for the party" were the judgments that seemed to define me. It was as though not having something gave others the right to mistreat me.

But I won't let that narrative linger because I bounced back from those hardships. I discovered my strength, and it was fueled by a growing faith that I didn't fully understand at the time.

My leftover feelings of abandonment and inadequacy led me into the arms of John, who was clearly the wrong person for me. On the surface, it seemed like he was looking out for me, offering "fashion advice" when he constantly asked for pictures of what I was planning on wearing that day or telling me what perfume I should use. But as time went on, it became clear that his intentions were more controlling than caring.

He would comment on the neckline of my clothing, suggesting it was too low and that I shouldn't send the wrong message. He questioned the type of perfume I used, even if it was a gift from another continent. It began to feel like every aspect of my appearance and choices was under scrutiny.

Then came the unwarranted advice about my diet and

health. He would criticize my food choices, claiming that certain foods were "fattening" and that I needed to focus on vitamins and supplements to manage my sugar levels. It was as if he was trying to dictate what I should eat and how I should take care of my health.

Initially, I thought he was genuinely concerned about my well-being, and I went along with their suggestions. However, over time, I began to see a pattern of control and manipulation. It was frustrating to realize that his intentions were not rooted in genuine care but rather in a desire to exert control over my choices and decisions.

When I resisted his advice and attempted to assert my own autonomy, it often led to arguments and frustration on his part. It became clear that his actions were not driven by love or protection but by a need to control and influence my life according to his preferences.

These experiences taught me the importance of recognizing when someone's actions, even if masked as protection or love, may actually be attempts to control or manipulate. It reinforced the need to trust my own judgment and make choices that are genuinely in my best interest rather than succumbing to external pressures or undue influence.

As an adult, I found it challenging to fully engage in social gatherings and to trust people, even when they hadn't given me any reason not to. The foundation of skepticism had been laid, and it made it difficult for me to let my guard down. I could be a good friend, but old traumas and unhealed emotions would resurface, pushing me back into a mode of isolation as a coping mechanism rather than a path to healing.

It was during my journey into adulthood that I turned to

God for guidance and solace. I realized that I couldn't continue living with this sense of isolation and mistrust. There was nothing inherently wrong with enjoying simple things like having lunch with someone or engaging in a healthy relationship. However, my past experiences had led me to be overly cautious, even accusatory, when it came to potential partners.

I recall a time when I was dating, and I found myself looking for signs of control in someone, even when they exhibited no such traits. I would accuse them of having hidden agendas, and unsurprisingly, these relationships didn't last long. It became evident that I couldn't maintain a healthy connection with others until I addressed the deep wounds within myself.

Ultimately, I had to choose between perpetuating the cycle of mistrust and isolation or embarking on a path of self-healing. It was a difficult decision, but I knew that I needed to prioritize my own well-being and work on changing my perception of love and relationships. I understood that I had the power to break free from the past and create healthier, more fulfilling connections with others, but it would require inner healing and a shift in my perspective.

Chapter 3: The Winds of Change

Right Place, Right Time— The Turning Point That Sparked Change

"Strengthening the disciples and encouraging them to re-main true to the faith. "We must go through many hardships to enter the kingdom of God," they said. "

Acts 14:22

Before the winds of change swept through the corridors of my life, I found myself on the precipice of complacency, naively mistaking the bars of my cage for the protective arms of a guardian. There I was, in the company of John, a man whose love language was laced with the syntax of pos-session. To the untrained eye, his attentiveness appeared as the hallmark of a devoted partner, his every action seem-ingly rooted in a deep concern for my well-being. In this illusion, I played the part of the cherished, unaware that with each passing day, my wings were being clipped under the guise of safeguarding my flight.

The moment of liberation did not arrive with the fanfare of epiphanies that novels often romanticize. Instead, it was a silent coup, a quiet realization that dawned on me in the most mundane of moments. The act of breaking away from John did not just signify the end of a tumultuous chapter but marked the beginning of a new age. I rediscovered the simple freedoms I had unwittingly relinquished— the liberty to adorn myself in attire that reflected my mood rather than his approval, the autonomy to indulge in food of my choosing, and the sheer bliss of crafting a life dictated by my own desires and whims. This transformative experience was not just about finding myself; it was about celebrating the very essence of my being, unfiltered and unrestrained.

In the unassuming crevices of an ordinary life, seismic shifts often come quietly, germinating in the soil of the mundane. My seismic shift happened on an inconspicuous Tuesday evening, the kind that had always promised the comfort of predictability but instead became the cradle of my emancipation. It felt like the walls around me were constantly closing in on me, the air heavy with the scent of a perfume I never chose—a subtle, yet constant, reminder of my shackled autonomy.

With John, life had settled into a rhythm that mimicked harmony to the undiscerning observer. It was during one such unremarkable conversation, woven with the banalities of everyday life, that a spark ignited within me. The dialogue itself was as it had always been—safe, superficial, yet underscored by the puppeteer's strings that John so expertly controlled. I was halfway through a sentence about something trivial when it struck me—the magnitude of his influence. Each word I spoke, each choice I made, was invisibly vetted by his standards, including the floral notes of perfume that clung to my skin, a fragrance I wore like a symbol of his sovereignty over my preferences, my identity, my essence.

It was in this flash of ordinary dialogue that something deep within the recesses of my spirit snapped—a threadbare rope giving way under the weight of suppressed individuality. The moment didn't arrive with the drama of clashing cymbals or the crescendo of a symphony. It was silent and reflective, a crack in the dam of my subservience through which my true self began to seep out, insistent and bold.

The clock ticked its usual rhythm, the room held its familiar form, and there sat John, the unwitting catalyst of my awakening, unaware that the very foundations of our existence were shifting under the weight of my newfound resolve.

As I stood there, a participant and a spectator in my own life, the realization crystalized with startling clarity. I had become ensnared in the age-old conundrum of sunk cost versus the priceless breath of freedom. I had spent several years, emotions, and fragments of myself invested in this relationship were the chains, mistaking for adornments. The countless compromises, the small concessions—I had packaged them neatly as the necessary give-and take of love. But here, in the quiet aftermath of my awakening, they revealed themselves as the steep payments towards a debt I never owed.

The realization was not merely an understanding but a palpable force, a tidal wave that washed over the debris of justifications I had built around me. It was a moment of reckoning with the truth that my autonomy was never meant to be bartered, that the investment of my self-worth in a joint stock with John was a venture that would never yield the dividends of true happiness.

In the immediacy of the moment, I felt an overwhelming sense of suffocation, as if the very air I breathed was filtered through a mesh woven by John's expectations. The walls, the scent, the ambient sounds of our shared life—it all converged into a cacophony of imprisonment. I felt the tightness in my chest, the same constriction that accompanies one who is about to dive into the unknown depths of an uncharted sea.

At the time of my awakening, the fabric of my day-to-day life was interwoven with John's, each thread a mingling of shared experiences and expectations. Socially, I can see in hindsight how I had become entangled in a world of secret desires and truths that couldn't be voiced. Our relationship, hidden in the shadows, kept me from enjoying simple pleasures, like bringing him to family gatherings. He wasn't mine to introduce openly, leaving me feeling awkward and isolated among my relatives.

This secret came at a high cost. It wasn't just about missing the chance to be seen together; it meant losing out on many public events because he was never available. As I reflect on this part of my life, it's important to capture not just the secrecy but also the emotional journey that follows. What started as light-hearted and carefree grew into something heavier and more complex.

Over time, the truth dawned on me. I was waiting for a commitment that would never come. My heart had confused lust for love, a mistake that still stings. I spent years, precious time, and so much of my emotional space on a yes that was never going to happen.

But there was a pivotal moment of change. God stepped in and freed me from this entanglement. It was a path to liberation, though not without its painful reminders. The hurt from what I thought was love still echoes, serving as a reminder of a past journey. But in that hurt, there is also a clear sense of freedom and the ever-present strength of faith.

Emotionally, I had navigated myself into a stillwater, seemingly calm but stagnant. Beneath the surface, my emotions were a kaleidoscope in muted shades, dulled by the constant censorship imposed by the relationship's dynamic. Smiles were often rehearsed, and laughter echoed with a hollowness that seemed to bounce off the walls of my chest, yearning for the resonance of authenticity.

The turning point was a crucible of emotions. Surprise at my own capacity for self-realization was tinged with embarrassment for not having recognized my predicament sooner. There was a surge of anger, too, a fierce, protective indignation on behalf of the 'me' that had been sidelined, shadowed by a partner's dominating will.

These emotions did not exist in isolation—they clashed, they merged, they competed for dominance in a relentless dance. Yet, in their collision, they created a harmony of purpose. The dissonance between what I had accepted and what I now realized I deserved played out in my mind like a symphony reaching its crescendo. The once suppressed parts of myself began to stir, to stretch their limbs, to find their voice.

The anger gave me strength, the embarrassment evolved into resolve, the hope carved out the path for courage, and fear became the adversary I was now equipped to face. This was not the discord of a life falling apart but the harmonious acknowledgment of a spirit preparing to rebuild. And within this emotional orchestra, a melody emerged— the song of self-liberation, playing the notes that would guide me toward a future written by my hand, my heart, my choices.

My goals, once entwined with John's, now demanded independence—the ambition to forge a path defined by my passions and curiosities rather than the expectations of a partnership that had lost its balance. The way I viewed relationships, the dynamics of power within them, and the importance of mutual respect and individuality underwent a rigorous, transformative scrutiny.

This moment of intense personal revelation rippled outward, influencing my broader worldview. I became more aware of the subtle dynamics of control and dependency that pervade many aspects of society. Empathy for others in similar situations swelled within me, as did a newfound appreciation for the importance of personal agency and self-advocacy. I started to perceive the world not as a fixed reality, but as a canvas upon which I could paint their own trajectories, unbound by the expectations and designs of others.

In the immediate wake of my realization, my actions were both instinctive and symbolic. I discarded the perfume—a liquid chain—and in this small, defiant act, I felt the first rush of liberation. Next, I initiated conversations that had been long overdue, discussions that were raw and honest, marking the end of an era with John and the beginning of a truthful dialogue with myself.

Planning for the future took on a dual essence; it was practical and dream-laden. I started laying the groundwork for independence—financial, social, and emotional. I sought counsel, reconnecting with old friends and forging new alliances with those who resonated with my newfound ideals. I crafted a vision for my life that was anchored in self-respect and the pursuit of happiness on my own terms.

I sketched out goals that were mine alone—career aspirations, personal development objectives, and milestones that celebrated individual achievement. The potential paths were not just different in direction but in destination. To relocate was to immerse myself in a new
context, ripe with the challenges and growth that come from uncharted territories and relationships. To reconnect with old friends and family was to embrace healing and the rediscovery of a support network that had been neglected. Choosing solitude was to embark on an intimate odyssey of self, to build a fortress of self-reliance before inviting the world back in.

Each path presented its unique terrain of risks and rewards, demanding careful consideration of how each choice would shape not only the narrative of my life but the core of who I was becoming.

As I confronted the spectrum of choices that fanned out before me, there were voices of doubt, legacies of the old me—a chorus cautioning against the hazards of the unknown. These were the whispers of a comfort zone that had become a prison, yet one whose bars I had grown to find reassuring in their familiarity.

Externally, there were tangible constraints. Finances, for one, demanded pragmatic consideration. There were also the expectations of those around me, the silent pressures of societal norms, and the daunting task of explaining my newfound direction to those who knew me as I was, not as I wished to become.

Overcoming these fears was no singular act of heroism but

a daily, gritty endeavor. It required a consistent application of faith in myself and the understanding that fear was a natural companion to change, not an enemy. I leaned into the discomfort, acknowledging its presence but refusing to grant it dominion over my actions.

I cultivated my own strength, using each small victory, each day I moved forward in spite of fear, as a building block for confidence. I reached out to mentors, to stories of others who had walked similar paths, and to the quiet but indomitable voice within that assured me of my capability.

I reframed failure not as a cataclysm but as a teacher, a pivot point from which to learn and adapt. In this reimagining of my journey, each fear I confronted and moved beyond was a triumph, proof to the human spirit's capacity to evolve. With every step taken in defiance of fear, I was not just moving towards something new—I was becoming someone new. The very act of facing the unknown and not receding was itself a form of success, proof that the only failure I had to fear was the failure to try.

The growth I experienced can be likened to the unfurling of leaves in spring, each new layer pushing through the soil of the past, reaching for the sun. With every uncomfortable step, I grew more in tune with myself, my needs, and my desires. The growth was not just emotional or psychological but spanned the breadth of my existence.

Professionally, I blossomed, my resume now dotted with the fruits of risks taken—roles I would have never applied for before, projects initiated from my own visions. Socially, my circle reflected a more diverse, vibrant collection of souls, each connection fostered through a willingness to be vulnerable and authentic.

Throughout this journey of self-discovery, there were poignant instances that pierced the veil of newfound confidence, moments when I was acutely reminded of my history of being second in line for consideration. There were dinner invitations declined in favor of more pressing engagements, and professional opportunities passed over, subtly implying that my talents were overshadowed by others'. Each instance was a small echo of the past, a reminder of what it felt like to not be the priority.

I recall the mixed emotions when seeing friends couple off, leaving me the odd one out, reinforcing a familiar pang of exclusion. Even within the family, sometimes I felt like an afterthought, receiving news of gatherings I was not invited to or decisions made without my input. These slights, though small in isolation, compiled a narrative that forced me to confront the unsettling question: what did it mean when others did not choose me?

The pain of these experiences often led to a cascade of introspection, where feelings of inadequacy would loom large. The internal dialogue was laced with self-doubt, questioning my worthiness, my capabilities, and my place in the social fabric that seemed at times to unravel at the edges.

I grappled with the corrosive thought that perhaps I was fundamentally lacking, that there was a flaw at the core of my being that rendered me unworthy of being chosen. Self-doubt would weave its insidious threads through my thoughts, a silent saboteur that threatened the foundations of the self-esteem I had fought so hard to rebuild.

Coping with the consistent realization that I was often a plan B, an option rather than a priority, was an arduous journey. At times, the silence of a phone that didn't ring or a message that went unread was louder than any direct rejection. It brought forth an intimate kind of anguish, a cocktail of confusion and self-questioning.

During these times, I turned to various forms of solace and reflection—journaling my thoughts, seeking the unbiased perspective of therapy, and leaning into the arts as a form of expression. These outlets provided a conduit for the pain, transforming it from a weight that threatened to drown me into a buoy that helped me stay afloat.

The ascent to a place where external validation ceased to be the cornerstone of my self-worth was steep and treacherous. It required the dismantling of long-held beliefs and the construction of a new framework for self-appreciation—one built on the recognition of my own accomplishments, the acceptance of my imperfections, and the celebration of my individuality.

Understanding the complexities of unspoken rejections required a honing of intuition and a cultivation of emotional intelligence. It was often in what was not said—in averted gazes, in the spaces between words, in the energy of a room—that I found the map to navigate these silent dismissals.

Accepting that not all answers would come in clear, articulate refusals, I learned to listen to the quieter frequencies of communication, to the subtext that said more than the text ever could. This tuning in was not about seeking signs of rejection in every interaction but about recognizing when a door was closed, so I could redirect my energies toward ones that were open.

To move past the silent "no," I adopted several strategies. I practiced detachment, understanding that my self-worth was not hinged on the approval or acceptance of others. I invested in self-improvement, focusing on personal and professional development that would open new avenues independent of others' validation.

I also embraced networking, understanding that each "no" could be a step towards a "yes" in a different sphere. The expansion of my social and professional circles introduced me to a diversity of opportunities, some of which were more aligned with my aspirations than those I had originally sought.

Moreover, I made a conscious effort to cultivate gratitude for the doors that did open and for the people who welcomed me with a "yes." This practice grounded me in positivity, keeping me focused on the abundance of opportunities around me, rather than the scarcity implied by rejection.

Navigating through the unspoken "no" became less about overcoming a barrier and more about following a detour, one that often led to vistas more breathtaking than I had imagined on my original path.

The turning point was not just a moment in time but the beginning of a lifelong exploration into the depths of my soul. And from this exploration, the value of embracing change has become my North Star, guiding me through the murky waters of uncertainty to the shores of self-realization.

Chapter 4: The Unseen Paths

Journey Through Choice and Acceptance – Divine Intervention

"For I know the plans I have for you," declares the Lord, "plans to prosper you and not to harm you, plans to give you hope and a future."

Jeremiah 29:11

In my life's journey, there came a pivotal moment, a decisive point where I stood at a crossroads. This wasn't just about picking a path; it was about facing the consequences of years spent in denial and half-hearted commitments. I had ignored the subtle nudges and louder calls that were meant to steer me towards a truer course. God had been tugging at my heart, yet I resisted, stubborn in my ways, entangled in a web of my own making.

It all revolved around personal choices – mine, and how they clashed or harmonized with divine guidance. I often found myself arguing with my conscience, rebuffing the internal voice that echoed with wisdom beyond my understanding. "You've done too much," it would accuse, or "You knew better but never fully stopped." These thoughts haunted me, echoing in the quiet moments, making me feel like a letdown in God's eyes.

But then, there were these moments of clarity, little miracles that couldn't be anything but signs. It was a test of faith, a battle between practical concerns and a deeper call to generosity. This wasn't an isolated incident. From IHOP to pawn shops, I found myself being guided to perform acts of kindness, each a lesson in obedience, no matter how small.

These experiences, though they seemed minor, were significant. They were lessons, God's way of showing me that true obedience often comes in small packages. However, I was so focused on my own turmoil that I often missed the point. It took me a while to realize that my reluctance to fully embrace God's path was hindering my own growth.

I was living in a fantasy, a maze of my own creation, where I convinced myself that I could manage everything alone. But it was God who was guiding me, gently, persistently. The realization hit me hard when I finally decided to cut off contact with someone who had become an unhealthy fixation in my life. That decision, as hard as it was, felt like breaking free from chains. It was a declaration of my choice to walk with God, to prioritize my spiritual journey over fleeting desires.

This choice wasn't just about turning away from a harmful relationship; it was a stepping stone towards self-discovery. For so long, I had defined myself through others – through my children, through the men in my life, through societal expectations. Now, it was time to find out who Connie really was, independent of these external influences.

I began to explore my likes and dislikes, to understand what it truly meant to be God's child. This process was about more than just self-improvement; it was about learning to trust in God's plan for me. I realized that being single wasn't a sentence to loneliness; it was an opportunity to build a deeper, more meaningful relationship with God. It dawned on me that if I had God with me, I had everything I needed.

As I look back, I see the missed opportunities, the times I felt alone in a crowd, the lack of meaningful connections. Yet, I also see the growth, the strength I found in my faith, and the peace that comes with surrendering to God's will. My journey hasn't been easy, but it's been transformative, and I hope it serves as a reminder to others that it's never too late to choose a path of faith and self-realization.

I often found myself in a tug-of-war between my inner conflicts and the subtle, yet persistent, divine signs that sought to guide me. This portion of my journey was marked by a deep struggle with feelings of unworthiness and a litany of past mistakes that seemed to weigh heavily on my soul.

For years, I grappled with a relentless sense of inadequacy. Each mistake I made felt like a black mark on my record, a record to my failings. "Too far gone," I'd often tell myself, believing that I had strayed too far from the path of righteousness to ever find my way back. These feelings of unworthiness were like shackles, holding me back from embracing the fullness of God's love and forgiveness.

Amidst this turmoil, there were signs – gentle, almost imperceptible nudges from the divine. But more often than not, I chose to ignore them, or I struggled to understand their significance. These signs came in various forms: a chance encounter, a line in a sermon that felt like it was spoken directly to me, or the unexplained comfort I felt in moments of quiet prayer. Yet, my skepticism and self-doubt often clouded my ability to see these for what they truly were – divine interventions.

I recall times when I would dismiss these moments as mere coincidences or ignore them entirely, convinced that I was unworthy of such guidance. The idea that God could still be reaching out to me, despite my past, seemed far-fetched. I questioned why a divine entity would bother with someone who had repeatedly turned away from His teachings. This internal battle only served to amplify my feelings of unworthiness.

However, it was through this very struggle that I began to understand the nature of God's grace. The more I confronted my inner conflicts, the clearer it became that these divine signs were not conditional upon my perfection. They were reminders of unconditional love, of a presence that remained steadfast regardless of how far I thought I had strayed.

Learning to acknowledge and accept these signs was a slow process. It involved shedding layers of guilt and self-condemnation, and gradually opening my heart to the possibility that I was still worthy of divine attention. This realization didn't come all at once, but unfolded gradually as I began to see the patterns in my life – the way certain experiences seemed to draw me back towards a spiritual path.

This part of my journey taught me the power of self-forgiveness and the importance of being open to the subtle ways in which the divine communicates with us. It was a lesson in humility and the understanding that our past mistakes do not define us in the eyes of God. By confronting my inner conflicts and learning to recognize the divine signs in my life, I was able to embark on a path of healing and spiritual growth, a journey towards a deeper understanding of myself and my place in the grand scheme of things.

Embarking on a journey beyond my comfort zones was akin to navigating uncharted waters. It was a path filled with uncertainty and fear, yet it was also a crucible for personal growth and an expression of faith. This stage of my life was about confronting the fears that had long held me captive, and making decisions that challenged my long-held beliefs and habits.

For years, my comfort zone had been a familiar, if not entirely happy, place. It was a space defined by routine, by the known and the predictable. Stepping out of it meant facing the unknown, confronting the fears that lurked in the shadows of change. The very thought of venturing into new territories, whether in my personal or spiritual life, filled me with apprehension. There was the fear of failure, the dread of judgment, and the nagging doubt about my own capabilities.

Yet, as I grew in my faith, I realized that remaining in my comfort zone was akin to stagnation. I was being called to step out, to trust in God's plan for me, even when it seemed daunting. This realization didn't make the journey easier, but it gave it purpose and direction. Each step outside my comfort zone was a leap of faith, a demonstration to my trust in divine guidance.

The decisions I had to make were often challenging. They ranged from altering long-standing relationships that were no longer serving me, to embracing new opportunities that I would have previously shunned out of fear. These decisions were accompanied by a tumult of emotions - anxiety, doubt, and sometimes, a sense of loss. But amidst these emotions, there was also a growing sense of empowerment and self-awareness.

One of the most reflective aspects of this journey was the personal growth that came with each challenging decision. With every step, I was learning more about myself - my strengths, my weaknesses, and my capacity for strength. These experiences taught me the value of courage, not the absence of fear, but the determination to move forward despite it.

This part of my path was also a deepening of my faith. Each challenge, each fear confronted, was a conversation with God, a reliance on His strength and wisdom. It was in these moments of vulnerability and uncertainty that I felt His presence most acutely, guiding and reassuring me.

In stepping out of my comfort zones, I discovered a version of myself that was braver, stronger, and more reliant on my faith than I ever knew possible. It was a journey that reshaped not just my external circumstances, but my inner landscape as well. I emerged from this process more attuned to my own needs and aspirations, and more importantly, with a deeper understanding of my relationship with God. It was a testament to the transformative power of faith and the courage to embrace change.

God blessed me with moments of divine intervention, often small and easy to overlook, were the nudges that steered me towards greater wisdom and understanding.

One such moment, etched vividly in my memory, is the grocery store incident. It was an ordinary day, filled with mundane tasks, but it turned into a lesson in empathy and obedience. As I was shopping, I ran into a cousin of my daughter. After a brief exchange, as I was about to leave, a quiet voice inside urged me to pay for her groceries. Initially, I hesitated, considering my own financial constraints. Yet, this nudge was persistent. When I eventually acted on it, the relief and gratitude in the young woman's eyes were a clear sign that I had done the right thing. This incident taught me the value of listening to those inner calls to kindness, no matter how small or inconvenient they might seem.

Another instance that comes to mind was a simple encounter at a local cafe. As I sat enjoying my coffee, I noticed an elderly man sitting alone, looking somewhat forlorn. Again, I felt a gentle push, an inner prompting to strike up a conversation with him. It turned out he was grieving the loss of his wife and craved human connection. Our conversation might have been brief, but the gratitude in his eyes spoke volumes. This experience reinforced my belief in the importance of being present and available for others, as God might be using me to provide comfort to someone in need.

Reflecting on these moments, I realized their immense significance in shaping my decisions and actions. They were not just random acts of kindness; they were deliberate prompts from God, guiding me to make a positive impact on the lives of others. These experiences helped me understand that divine intervention isn't always grand or dramatic. Sometimes, it's found in the quiet, everyday moments, nudging us towards acts of compassion and kindness.

Each of these encounters served as a reminder of the interconnectedness of our lives and the role faith can play in guiding our actions. They taught me to be more attuned to the needs of those around me, to listen more carefully to the quiet stirrings of my heart, and to trust that in doing so, I was aligning my actions with a greater, divine purpose. These small nudges were, in essence, God's way of reminding me that every action, no matter how insignificant it might seem, has the potential to bring light and love into the world.

In life, we often face the stark reality of not being chosen – be it in relationships, careers, or various opportunities. Rejection, in any form, carries with it a deep sense of pain and inadequacy. For me, this was particularly poignant in my personal relationships. The sting of not being chosen, of being overlooked or deemed not enough, was a wound that cut deep. It brought forth a barrage of questions about my worth and desirability. "Why not me?" became a recurring, painful mantra, echoing my insecurities and doubts.

This emotional toll was not just about the immediate hurt; it seeped into other areas of my life, affecting my self-esteem and how I interacted with the world. It was a struggle, a constant battle between self-pity and the quest for understanding. Yet, in this struggle, there was also a journey towards acceptance and growth.

Accepting the unchosen path was not an easy feat. It required a deep introspection and a shift in perspective. Instead of viewing rejection as a reflection of my inadequacy, I began to see it as a redirection, a nudge towards a path better suited for me. This shift didn't happen overnight. It was a gradual process, facilitated by prayer, reflection, and a conscious effort to trust in God's plan.

As I navigated this path, I learned valuable lessons about self-worth and faith. My worth wasn't determined by others' inability to see my value. I realized that my identity and value were rooted in my relationship with God, not in the fleeting judgments of others. This understanding brought a sense of liberation and self-acceptance that was previously missing from my life.

Moreover, my faith played a crucial role in this journey. Believing that there was a divine reason behind every rejection, that God was guiding me towards something better, helped alleviate the sting of being unchosen. It gave me the strength to persevere, to remain hopeful, and to stay open to new possibilities.

In hindsight, the unchosen paths were instrumental in shaping me into the person I am today. They taught me tenacity, helped me develop a stronger sense of self, and deepened my faith.

Each rejection, each closed door, was a step towards discovering a path that was truly meant for me – one that led to greater fulfillment, peace, and understanding of my place in God's plan.

The next stage of my journey was marked by a shift in focus – from external relationships to internal exploration and a deeper communion with God.

For so long, my identity and sense of purpose were intertwined with my role as a parent and caretaker. However, as my children grew up and became independent, I was left with a void, a silence that demanded attention. This was both daunting and liberating. Daunting, because I had to confront questions about my own likes, dislikes, and aspirations, and liberating, because it was an opportunity to rediscover myself, to find out who Connie really was beyond her roles and responsibilities, as much as I love my children.

This process of self-discovery involved a journey into solitude – not loneliness, but a deliberate choice to spend time in introspection and conversation with God. In these moments of solitude, I found the space to explore my thoughts and feelings without distractions or external influences. It was a time to listen, to reflect, and to understand my true desires and needs.

As I delved deeper into this journey, I experienced a realization about my self-worth and identity. I came to understand that my value wasn't defined by my relationships or accomplishments but by my inherent worth as a child of God. This was a pivotal moment, a shift from seeking validation from others to embracing my identity as a "loyal child of God."

This newfound understanding of self-worth was empowering. It helped me to see that I was complete in myself, that my relationship with God was the most crucial connection I could cultivate. It brought a sense of peace and contentment that I had not known before. My solitude with God became a source of strength, a sacred space where I could recharge, reflect, and grow in faith.

Embracing this solitude also allowed me to develop a more intimate relationship with God. In the quiet, away from the noise and demands of everyday life, I could hear His voice more clearly, feel His presence more. It was in these moments that I received the greatest insights into my life's purpose and God's plan for me.

This period of self-discovery and embracing solitude with God was transformative. It not only provided clarity about who I was but also redefined my approach to life. It taught me that being alone didn't mean being lonely, and that true fulfillment and joy come from within, from a deep and abiding connection with the Divine. It was a journey that affirmed my identity, not just as an individual but as a beloved and loyal child of God.

For years, I grappled with the temptation of fleeting desires. Whether it was the pursuit of romantic relationships, material gains, or societal approval, I found myself constantly chasing things that offered momentary satisfaction but left me feeling empty in the long run. The turning point came when I recognized this cycle for what it was – a pursuit of temporary gratification that was diverting me from a deeper, more meaningful path.

Choosing faith over these desires was not an easy decision. It meant letting go of certain habits, relationships, and patterns of thinking that had become deeply ingrained. It required a level of honesty and introspection that was at times uncomfortable. But in this discomfort, there was growth and a gradual awakening to the lasting joy that comes from a life rooted in faith.

As I embarked on this new path, I found blessings and inner peace that had previously eluded me. The superficial highs of temporal desires were replaced by a sense of contentment and fulfillment that was steady and enduring. This wasn't the fleeting happiness that came from external sources; it was a deep-seated joy that emanated from my connection with God.

This choice brought with it a sense of freedom. Freed from the constant chase after ephemeral pleasures, I found myself more attuned to the spiritual aspects of my life. My priorities shifted, and I began to value experiences and relationships that nurtured my soul and brought me closer to God.

Moreover, this decision had a ripple effect on other areas of my life. My relationships became more meaningful, my choices more intentional, and my sense of purpose more defined. I began to see the world through a lens of gratitude and faith, appreciating the simple blessings that each day brought.

The inner peace that came with choosing faith over temporal desires was transformative. It was a peace that transcended external circumstances, a steady anchor in the tumultuous seas of life. It affirmed my belief that true happiness and contentment are found not in the fleeting pleasures of the world but in a life lived in harmony with one's spiritual beliefs. It was a reminder that while temporal desires may offer temporary satisfaction, it is in faith that we find lasting joy and peace.

Reflecting on my path, I see it marked by significant moments of doubt, fear, and change, all navigated with faith and a quiet strength. This path, while challenging, has led me to a deeper understanding and a sense of peace, highlighting the crucial role of divine guidance in overcoming life's hurdles and finding true contentment.

Each step, from confronting inner conflicts to making the pivotal choice to prioritize faith over temporary pleasures, has been an enlightening process. It taught me that being strong is not just enduring hardships, but growing through them with faith as a guiding force. The challenges I encountered were not mere roadblocks but catalysts for deepening my relationship with God and comprehending His plan for my life.

Divine guidance has been a constant in this process. In moments of uncertainty and decision making, it was this guidance that steered me towards making choices that were right for me, choices that brought a sense of fulfillment and alignment with my spiritual beliefs. This guidance wasn't always loud or clear; often, it was a whisper, a nudge in the right direction, a feeling of peace amidst chaos.

Wrapping up, I want to impart a message of hope and encouragement to others who might be facing similar struggles. This path, though fraught with challenges, is also filled with opportunities for growth, self-discovery, and a deeper connection with the divine. The key is to remain open to divine guidance, to trust in the process, and to believe in the possibility of a future shaped by faith.

Embracing this future with faith means accepting that while we may not always understand the twists and turns of our path, there is a greater plan at work, one that leads to true happiness and fulfillment. It's about moving forward with the confidence that comes from knowing you are guided, loved, and supported every step of the way.

Chapter 5: Embracing the Journey

A Step Towards Faith and Hope— Finding Light

"And we know that for those who love God all things work together for good, for those who are called according to his purpose. "

Romans 8:28

My childhood, while sprinkled with moments of innocence and joy, was primarily a labyrinth of struggles. The bullying at school, the sneers and the scissors cutting through my self-worth, were not just incidents but defining moments. These trials, though harsh, were my first teachers. They instilled in me a strength that became the bedrock of my character. The emotional armor I built wasn't just a shield; it was my initiation into a life of overcoming adversity.

The journey through my relationships, particularly with John, was like navigating through a storm with no compass. It was a dance of self-discovery, where each step taken was a lesson in understanding love, worth, and the importance of self-autonomy. The realization that I was more than an option in someone else's life, that I was worthy of a love that was all mine, marked a turning point. It was a painful yet necessary awakening to my own value.

Every challenge I faced, be it in school, in relationships, or within myself, was like a cocoon. Emerging from it wasn't just about survival; it was about transformation. Every tear shed, every night spent in prayer, was a stitch in the fabric of my growth. It was in these moments of solitude and reflection that I discovered the essence of who I am – worthy, and continually evolving.

Perhaps the most deep journey has been my spiritual awakening. Each verse of scripture that resonated in the depths of my soul, every prayer whispered in the quiet of the night, has been a step closer to God. This spiritual journey has been my beacon, guiding me through tumultuous seas, offering solace in times of despair, and illuminating the path of true self discovery.

In reflection, each struggle, each tear, and each moment of doubt was a necessary chapter in my story. They were not just trials but invitations from the divine, urging me to grow, to learn, and to embrace the fullness of my being. As I stand here, looking back at the journey, I see not just a series of events but a mosaic of divine intervention and unceasing growth.

Reflecting on my past, the varied experiences of my life paint a portrait of growth, faith, and endurance. Each stage, with its unique trials and triumphs, has woven the fabric of my being, molding me into the person I am today.

My early years, marked by a multitude of struggles, were not merely a series of unfortunate events, but a crucible where my spirit was tempered. The taunts and isolation I faced were not just scars but also guiding stars, leading me towards strength. These early challenges taught me that true strength lies in the courage to continue despite vulnerability.

The turbulent journey of love and loss, especially with John, was not just a painful chapter but a significant teacher. Through this emotional upheaval, I learned the critical importance of self worth. These experiences reflected back to me a woman deserving of a love that elevates, not diminishes. I discovered that the foundation of love lies in first valuing oneself.

Each challenge I encountered was a transformative stage, where I emerged not unscathed, but more grounded, more genuine. These experiences charted the course of my personal development, teaching me that change, though often difficult, is essential for personal evolution.

The most transformative aspect has been my spiritual journey. In moments of despair, my faith acted as a light, guiding me through life's storms. My spirituality is the lens through which I view my existence, teaching me that every challenge is an opportunity for growth and a deeper connection with the divine.

Piecing these experiences together reveals a story of a woman transformed by her trials, strengthened by her faith, and anchored in her true self. The lessons learned have not just shaped my identity; they have redefined it. Where once stood a girl overshadowed by adversity, now stands a woman illuminated by grace, endurance, and an unbreakable belief in herself.

In this reflection, I find not just closure but also gratitude for the journey. It is through these myriad experiences that I have discovered who I am - a strong spirit, a compassionate heart, and a soul in constant pursuit of growth and divine connection.

In the winding journey of my life, faith has been the light-house, guiding me through the darkest nights and storm-iest seas. It has been a source of strength, not just in times of trouble, but as a constant, steady flame illuminating my path.

From the earliest days of my childhood, through the tu-mult of adolescence and into the complexities of adult-hood, faith has been my anchor. In moments when the world seemed too overwhelming, when the weight of my struggles threatened to break me, it was faith that offered solace and strength. It taught me to see beyond the imme-diate pain, to understand that every trial is transient and every challenge an opportunity to grow stronger in spirit.

My faith journey has been one of learning to trust - not just in a higher power, but in the plan that this power has for me. It taught me to surrender control, to understand that while I may not always understand the path I am on, there is a purpose to every twist and turn.

There have been moments in my life where the hand of di-vine intervention was unmistakable. Times when clarity cut through confusion like a beacon of light, offering direc-tion and purpose when I needed it most.

Each of these moments, whether they came during quiet contemplation in prayer or as sudden epiphanies in the midst of chaos, were pivotal. They were not just moments of realization but of transformation. These were the times when my faith not only provided answers but also re-shaped my questions, leading me towards deeper under-standing and insight.

The realizations borne from my faith have been more than just personal truths; they have been guideposts, directing me towards a life of greater purpose and fulfillment. They taught me to embrace my journey with an open heart and a trusting spirit, knowing that even when the path is unclear, I am being led in the right direction.

Throughout my journey, change has been a constant companion, sometimes as a gentle guide, at other times as a forceful catalyst. Embracing change, I've learned, is not merely about acceptance; it is about recognizing its essential role in personal growth and evolution.

Change, with all its uncertainty and unpredictability, has often felt like a dance with the unknown. There were moments when it swept me off my feet, and times when it challenged my every step. But in this dance, I found rhythm and grace. I learned that in the heart of change lies opportunity – the chance to shed old skins, to grow, to renew oneself.

Each chapter of change, whether it unfolded through personal struggles, shifting relationships, or spiritual awakening, has been transformative. It has taught me to be adaptable, and most importantly, to be open to the lessons that come with new beginnings and endings. Embracing change has meant embracing growth in its most authentic form.

As I navigated the twists and turns of my life, I realized the impact of personal choices. Every decision, every crossroad, has been instrumental in shaping the contours of my destiny.

Life is a journey full of choices, difficult choices that we must make, with each piece reflecting a decision, a turning point, a moment of clarity. Making conscious choices has meant taking ownership of my journey, acknowledging that while I may not control every aspect of my life, the power to choose my response, my attitude, and my actions lies solely with me.

Choosing consciously has required courage – the courage to face the unknown, to step out of comfort zones, and to confront the possibility of failure. Yet, it is through these choices that I have discovered my strengths, honed my values, and carved out a path that is uniquely mine.

As I stand at the precipice of the future, the lessons learned from my past experiences cast a guiding light on the path ahead. My aspirations for the future are deeply rooted in these valuable lessons, shaping a vision that is both hopeful and grounded in reality.

My dreams for the future are not mere flights of fancy but are infused with the wisdom gleaned from each challenge and triumph. I aspire to continue my journey with the same courage and faith that have brought me this far, seeking opportunities that not only promise personal fulfillment but also contribute to the greater good.

Looking forward, I envision a life where my personal and spiritual growth translates into meaningful impact. Whether it be through writing, speaking, or community engagement, I aim to share the insights and experiences that have shaped my journey, hoping to inspire and empower others on their own paths.

The journey of personal growth and spiritual development is not one with a finite end. It is an ongoing process, a commitment to continuous learning and evolving.

I recognize that the road ahead will be filled with new challenges and opportunities for learning. Embracing these as part of the journey, I commit to remaining open to new experiences, ideas, and perspectives, knowing that each will contribute to my growth.

My spiritual journey, a cornerstone of my life, is an ever-deepening well of wisdom and strength. I am committed to nurturing this connection, understanding that it is a vital source of guidance and peace in the face of uncertainties in life.

My journey, full of trials and triumphs, is not just my story; it is a ray of encouragement for others. In sharing my experiences, I aim to empower those who may find themselves walking similar paths, offering them the assurance that they are not alone in their struggles.

There is power in shared experiences, in knowing that someone else has navigated the same turbulent waters and emerged stronger. My intention is to offer that sense of connection and understanding, to light a path of hope for others. The lessons I've learned in bravery, faith, and self-discovery are not just personal triumphs but are messages of strength for anyone seeking guidance.

Empowerment comes from understanding – understanding that challenges are not roadblocks but stepping stones, that every struggle is an opportunity for growth. By sharing my story, I hope to inspire others to embrace their journey with courage and optimism, to recognize their own strength and potential.

In hindsight, the wisdom I've gathered is not just a treasure trove of personal insights but a legacy I wish to share with my readers.

Life, in all its complexity, has taught me invaluable lessons. The importance of embracing change, the power of making conscious choices, the strength that comes from faith, and the transformative impact of personal growth – these are the cornerstones of wisdom I wish to pass on.

This wisdom, hard-earned and deeply cherished, is offered as a guiding light. To the reader who may find themselves in the throes of hardship or at the crossroads of decision, these insights are a compass, pointing towards hope, and the endless possibilities that life offers.

I am finding myself at a crossroads of memory and anticipation, where the past converges with the future. This journey, marked by its diverse chapters of trials and triumphs, has not just been a passage through time but a transformation of my very being.

Looking back, I see a mosaic of experiences, each piece distinct yet integral to the whole. From the early days of childhood struggles, where I first learned the harsh realities of life, to the complexities of relationships that taught me the value of self-worth and love, each step has been transformative. These experiences were not just events; they were the crucibles in which my character was forged, shaping me into the woman I stand as today.

The past has been a masterful teacher, imparting lessons through each joy and sorrow. I learned bravery in the face of adversity, faith in moments of despair, and the power of choice in shaping my destiny. These lessons have become the guiding principles of my life, a compass that directs my decisions and actions.

My faith and spirituality have been the bedrock upon which my life is built. They have offered solace in times of trouble, strength in moments of weakness, and clarity when confusion reigned. This spiritual journey has been the thread that weaves through the fabric of my experiences, connecting each one with a deeper purpose and meaning.

Change and choice have been constant companions on my journey. Embracing change has taught me the beauty of adaptability and growth, while making conscious choices has empowered me to take control of my narrative. These elements have not just shaped my journey; they have defined it, teaching me that life is not just about what happens to us, but how we respond to it.

As I look towards the future, I do so with a heart full of hope and a mind rich with aspirations. The lessons of the past are the foundation upon which I build my dreams. I see a future where my experiences continue to guide me, where personal and spiritual growth remains at the forefront of my endeavors.

My journey, shared with honesty and vulnerability, is a testament to the enduring spirit of the human heart. It is a message of hope to those who may be navigating their own turbulent paths, a reminder that out of hardship can come strength, out of despair can come faith, and out of confusion can come clarity.

As I stand here, at this juncture between what has been and what is yet to come, I look ahead with optimism. The future, with all its unknowns, is not a source of fear but a canvas of possibility. It is an invitation to continue growing, learning, and evolving. I step forward with the knowledge that the best of my journey is not behind me but ahead, waiting to be discovered and embraced.

This journey, my journey, is a testament to the power of the human spirit to overcome, to evolve, and to thrive. It is a narrative of hope, and the unending quest for growth and fulfillment. As I look to the future, I do so not just with hope but with the certainty that whatever it holds, I am ready to meet it with the same courage, faith, and openness that have brought me this far.

Chapter 6: Ascending from the Abyss

Converting Suffering into Victory — Navigating Obstacles and Pitfalls

"Keep your life free from love of money, and be content with what you have, for he has said, 'I will never leave you nor forsake you.'"

Hebrews 13:5-6

As I embark on narrating this pivotal chapter of my life, it is essential to glance back at the winding roads I've traversed. The previous chapters of my story have painted a picture of adversities and personal challenges, each one pulled from the fabric of my being. From the raw exposure of my vulnerabilities to the stark confrontations with life's harsh realities, these experiences have been both my crucible and my chrysalis.

In these early pages, I recounted moments of heartache and confusion, the times when I felt lost in a labyrinth of emotions and circumstances. There were days when the dawn seemed like a distant dream, and nights that stretched endlessly, shrouded in the cloak of my solitude and despair. Yet, each chapter served as a stepping stone, a necessary passage through the shadowed valleys of my journey.

As we step into this chapter, there is a perceptible shift in the air. It's time to pivot from the narrative of struggles to one of transformation and growth. This is not just a recounting of what was, but a celebration of what is to be. It is about metamorphosis – a journey from the depths of despair to the heights of triumph.

The stories and reflections that follow are more than just remnants of a troubled past; they are the seeds of a future replete with hope. They are a testament to the power of the human spirit to overcome, to find meaning in the midst of turmoil, and to emerge stronger, wiser, and more grounded.

In this chapter, I invite you to walk with me as I transform pain into motivation, adversity into opportunity, and trials into triumphs. Together, we will explore how the darkest moments can lead to the most illuminating realizations, and how, in the grand scheme of life, every event has its purpose, every color its place. Welcome to a story of rebirth, a narrative of rising above, and a testament to the indomitable strength of faith and inner strength.

I'm delving into the heart of my journey, exploring the stark adversities that have shaped my path.

One of the most significant of these was the harrowing realization of being ensnared in a deceptive relationship. This revelation was not just a single moment of clarity, but a series of jolting awakenings that unraveled the illusions I had held onto.

The emotional impact of this discovery was akin to navigating a stormy sea. Feelings of betrayal, confusion, and heartbreak surged and ebbed, leaving me to grapple with a tumultuous inner world. Mentally, it was a battleground where trust warred with doubt, and reality clashed with illusion. The pain of deception cut deeply, challenging my perceptions of love, loyalty, and truth.

Amidst this turmoil, my faith became my anchor. It was not just a source of comfort, but a beacon of light guiding me through the fog of confusion. It gave me the strength to face the harsh truths and the courage to let go of the mirages that I had once cherished. My faith was a constant reminder that even in the midst of betrayal and pain, there is a path forward, a hope for healing and renewal.

Through these trials, my faith evolved, becoming more than a mere belief—it transformed into a lived experience, a tangible force that sustained me in my darkest hours. It taught me that endurance is not just about withstanding the storm, but also about finding the courage to step into the unknown, trusting that every challenge is a stepping stone to growth and understanding.

In confronting and overcoming these challenges, I learned invaluable lessons about the human heart, the complexities of relationships, and the unyielding power of faith to heal and transform. These experiences, though fraught with pain, were instrumental in shaping the person I am today—stronger, more empathetic, and imbued with a deeper understanding of life's dance between joy and sorrow.

In the narrative of my life, a pivotal moment came with the stark realization of the deceptive nature of a relationship that I had deeply invested in. This revelation was not just a fleeting insight; it was a seismic shift in my understanding of reality. The truth, when it unveiled itself, was not gentle. It tore through the fabric of what I believed, leaving me to confront the raw and unvarnished reality of betrayal.

The emotional aftermath of this discovery was tumultuous. A whirlwind of feelings engulfed me—anger, grief, disbelief—all swirling into a vortex of inner chaos. This was not merely a heartbreak; it was an existential crisis that called into question my judgments, my choices, and the very foundation of my trust. The introspection that followed was intense and unyielding. I found myself dissecting every memory, every word exchanged, seeking answers in the maze of past interactions.

In this crucible of confusion and pain, my spirituality became my compass. Proverbs 19, with its timeless wisdom, served as a guidepost, offering solace and perspective in a time of upheaval. These ancient words spoke to my situation with startling relevance, reminding me that human wisdom is fallible, but there is a greater truth and understanding that comes from a deeper, spiritual place.

This scripture helped me to detach, to view my situation from a higher vantage point. It was a lens that brought clarity amidst the blur of emotions, enabling me to see the bigger picture beyond my immediate pain. It taught me that discernment is not just about seeing things as they are, but understanding their deeper significance in the grand scheme of life.

In the light of Proverbs 19, time gradually unfolded a new perspective for me, one that was divinely guided. It was as though the Lord opened my eyes, allowing me to see the true essence of the person I had once idealized. The changes were subtle yet revealing. His once favored Nike sneakers were replaced by New Balance, a subtle symbol of the shifts that time brings. His manner of speaking transformed, now with only his bottom teeth showing, a stark contrast to the charm he once exuded.

The way he dressed underwent a change too; his shirts, which used to flow fashionably, were now neatly tucked in, conforming to a more conventional style. His physique also told a story of time's passage, marked by the inevitable bow of the belly. The man who once seemed to hang the moon in my sky now appeared to be a mere mortal, showing signs of a life lived and perhaps, lived hard.

This realization was akin to the ending of a long-held but misguided affection, captured perfectly by the Southern saying, "I loved his dirty underwear from last year." The list of overlooked faults and ignored signs had finally ceased. In this awakening, I found an unexpected gratitude and a sense of peace.

This peace was not just the absence of turmoil; it was an active, living presence in my life. It stemmed from the realization and acceptance that being alone did not equate to loneliness. In my solitude, I discovered the encompassing and love of God. The promise from God, "He'll never leave nor forsake us," resonated deeply with me, providing a constant reminder of His presence in my life.

This divine assurance brought a new understanding and a new form of contentment. It taught me that with God, I had everything I needed. The peace and love that I found in my faith were not just comforting; they were empowering. They allowed me to embrace life with a sense of completeness and fulfillment, grounded not in external validation or fleeting affections, but in the eternal and unchanging love of God.

The role of spirituality in this phase of my life was transformative. It was not just about finding comfort in faith;

it was about reorienting myself to a truth that transcended the immediate reality of my circumstances. It was a journey from confusion to clarity, from turmoil to tranquility. It was here that I learned the power of spirituality to illuminate the darkest corners of our experiences, guiding us towards a path of healing and understanding.

The journey of transforming pain into motivation has been a significant part of my narrative. In the wake of personal pain and acute disappointment, particularly from the deception I endured, I found myself at a crossroads. I could either remain mired in the anguish or use this pain as a catalyst for positive change. Choosing the latter, I embarked on a transformative path where my deepest sorrows became the impetus for my most significant actions and decisions.

This process began with a conscious decision to channel my emotional energy into constructive pursuits. Rather than allowing the pain to consume me, I redirected it towards self improvement, nurturing my talents, and pursuing goals that had long lain dormant. This shift was not immediate but was a gradual realignment of my priorities and perspective, turning every setback into a stepping stone towards personal growth and fulfillment. Amidst these experiences, I discovered an inner fortitude that I hadn't fully recognized before. Every challenge became an opportunity to strengthen this newfound strength. It was as if each trial polished and refined my character, uncovering layers of determination and courage that had been buried under the weight of past hurts.

One of the most significant shifts was moving away from seeking external validation to cultivating a deep sense of self-worth and faith. I learned to find validation not in the approval of others but in my own sense of integrity and the strength of my convictions. My faith, too, became a cornerstone in this journey, providing a sense of purpose and direction that was unshakable. It offered a sense of security and self-assurance that no external accolade could provide.

This transformative journey was not just about overcoming pain; it was about redefining my relationship with it. Pain, once a source of weakness, became a wellspring of motivation and a testament to the enduring human spirit's capacity to adapt, grow, and find meaning in the face of life's most challenging moments.

In my journey of self-discovery and healing, harnessing inner strength has been a crucial aspect. This chapter delves into the various techniques and practices that have been instrumental in this process, including prayer, reflection, and the support of a compassionate community.

Prayer has been the cornerstone of my journey towards inner strength. It provided a sanctuary of peace and clarity amidst the chaos of emotions and uncertainties. Through prayer, I found not just solace, but also the courage to face my fears and challenges head-on. It was in these moments of quiet communion that I gathered the strength to continue, even when the path ahead seemed insurmountable.

Reflection, too, played a vital role. It involved looking inward, examining my thoughts, emotions, and reactions to the events unfolding in my life. This process of introspection was not always easy; it required confronting uncomfortable truths and acknowledging my vulnerabilities. However, it was through this honest self-assessment that

I gained a deeper understanding of myself and my innate strength.

The support of my community was another pillar that bolstered my inner strength. Friends, family, and even acquaintances provided a network of support that was both uplifting and grounding. Their words of encouragement, acts of kindness, and presence were reminders that I was not alone in my struggles. This sense of belonging and connection was a powerful force that helped me navigate through the toughest times.

My journey of cultivating inner strength is dotted with numerous personal anecdotes. One such story is of a particularly challenging period when I felt overwhelmed by doubt and fear. It was during a quiet evening of reflection and prayer that I experienced peace and assurance. This moment was a turning point, reinforcing my belief in my own strength and the support of a higher power.

Reflecting on what kept me tethered to a falsehood is akin to standing in an endless line, waiting for a turn that never seemed to come. It was like playing a game of "That's my car," where I clung to a flickering hope, perhaps against better judgment. This hope was nurtured by promises and reassurances, which, in hindsight, were nothing more than carefully spun lies.

The truth, when it revealed itself, was a bitter pill to swallow. I discovered that not only was he married, but I was not the only other woman in his life. In this web of deceit, I was the extreme extra, a role that left me grappling with a sense of betrayal and self-doubt. In this game, where promises were the currency, he was the sole victor, playing his part with a skill that blinded me to reality.

As time progressed, his arrogance seemed to grow in proportion to the fading light of truth. The saying "Why buy the cow when the milk is free?" echoes painfully true in this context. My insecurities, perhaps, played a role in this prolonged charade. Years slipped by with little change in the pattern of our relationship or the level of affection shown. It was a cycle of hope and disappointment, a pattern I struggled to break.

Attempting to leave this toxic cycle was like trying to escape a powerful addiction. Each time I resolved to move on, a few unsuccessful dates would lead me back to him, as I found myself invariably comparing others to the illusion he represented. This cycle continued, a seemingly endless loop of return and regret.

However, the most astonishing part of this journey was how this cycle was broken. In what can only be described as a divine intervention, the shackles of this addiction were shattered in an instant. This moment of liberation was not just an end to a painful chapter but the beginning of a new understanding of faith and strength. It was a testament to the belief that sometimes, in our darkest and most entangled moments, a higher power can intervene in the most unexpected ways, illuminating a path to freedom and self-realization.

Another anecdote involves the support I received from a close friend during a time of despair. Their empathetic listening and wise counsel provided a new perspective and rekindled my hope and determination. These experiences, among others, are testaments to the growth of my inner fortitude, a journey marked by gradual but significant strides towards self-assurance and emotional stability.

Harnessing inner strength has been a multifaceted process,

nurtured by prayer, reflection, and the invaluable support of those around me. Each of these elements played a critical role in building a foundation of strength that has been essential in my journey of healing and personal growth.

The period of adversity I endured became a catalyst for remarkable achievements. One notable accomplishment was the newfound ability to channel my experiences into creative and constructive endeavors. This included writing, which not only served as a therapeutic outlet but also allowed me to connect with others who shared similar experiences. Additionally, I took bold steps in my professional life, embracing opportunities I previously would have shied away from, driven by a renewed sense of purpose and confidence.

These experiences reshaped my understanding of myself and my relationships. I learned to value my own worth and to recognize the importance of healthy, supportive connections with others. The realization that I deserved honesty and respect in my relationships led to a more selective and nurturing approach to the people I chose to surround myself with.
This period of transformation also brought about a deeper sense of self-awareness and emotional intelligence, enabling me to engage with others more empathetically and authentically.

Embracing a new identity and a refreshed perspective on life was perhaps the most significant change. This new identity was not defined by my past struggles but was a reflection of my journey towards healing and growth. It was an identity rooted in strength, self-respect, and an unshakeable belief in my capabilities. My perspective on life shifted dramatically; I began to see challenges not as insurmountable obstacles but as opportunities for growth and learning. This change in mindset opened up a world of possibilities, allowing me to live more boldly, with gratitude and a zest for life.

Rising above my circumstances involved a series of triumphs—both big and small—that collectively marked a period of significant personal evolution. These triumphs were not just milestones to be celebrated but were also instrumental in shaping a stronger, more self-assured, and optimistic version of myself, ready to embrace life with open arms and a hopeful heart.

These lessons have not only shaped my current life choices but also continue to influence my perspectives and personal development. One of the key takeaways from this journey is the power of embracing vulnerability. I learned that acknowledging and expressing my pain was not a sign of weakness, but a courageous step towards healing. This realization empowered me to face my fears and insecurities head-on, leading to a more authentic and fulfilling life.

Another significant lesson is the importance of self-care and setting healthy boundaries. My experiences taught me to prioritize my well-being and to recognize the value of saying no to situations and relationships that do not serve my best interests. This awareness has been instrumental in fostering a more balanced and harmonious life.

The transformative power of forgiveness was also a crucial insight. Forgiving those who wronged me, and importantly, forgiving myself, freed me from the chains of bitterness and regret. This act of forgiveness was not an endorsement of past wrongs but a release that allowed me to move forward with a lighter heart.

The ongoing role of faith and spirituality in my personal development has been intensive. My faith provided a steady source of comfort and guidance, helping me navigate through life's storms. It instilled a sense of hope and optimism, even in the darkest moments, and reminded me of the bigger picture and purpose of my life.

These lessons have significantly influenced my current life choices and perspectives. I now approach life with a more open and reflective mindset, valuing experiences for the growth they bring. My decisions are more aligned with my core values and beliefs, and I actively seek out opportunities that foster personal growth and contribute positively to my surroundings.

The journey from pain to triumph has been a rich learning experience, imparting lessons that continue to shape my life. These insights have not only transformed how I view myself and the world around me but have also reinforced the integral role of faith and spirituality in my ongoing journey of personal development and self-discovery.

As I draw the curtains on this chapter of my life, reflecting on the journey from 'the pit to the palace' evokes a myriad of emotions. This journey, marked by trials and triumphs, has been a testament to the spirit within me and the grace that has guided me through. Looking back, the path from deep despair to a place of strength and fulfillment was not linear. It was a journey filled with unexpected twists and turns, highs and lows, and lessons learned along the way. Yet, each step, each hurdle, has been integral in shaping the person I am today.

The importance of faith and self-belief in facing future challenges cannot be overstated. My faith has been the bedrock of my existence, a constant source of strength and hope. It has been the light that shone through the darkest times, reminding me that there is always a path forward, even when it seems hidden. This faith, coupled with a renewed belief in my abilities, has equipped me to face the uncertainties of life with a sense of assurance and optimism.

As I look towards the future, my heart is filled with hope and a deep-seated faith. The journey ahead is as much an unknown as it has always been, yet I step into it with a different perspective. Grounded in spirituality and self-awareness, I am now more attuned to the lessons each experience brings. I embrace the future, not just as a series of events to be lived, but as an opportunity for continued growth, learning, and fulfillment.

In closing, I would like to say that this journey from pain to empowerment has been transformative. It has shown me that within every challenge lies an opportunity for growth, and within every setback, a chance to come back stronger. With a heart full of gratitude and a spirit buoyed by faith, I am ready to embark on the next phase of my journey, carrying with me the lessons of the past and the hope of a brighter, more fulfilling future.

Chapter 7: Timeless Wisdom

Drawing Inspiration from the Old Testament

As I sit alone in the serenity of my small living room, the ancient pages of the Old Testament open on my lap, I find myself lost in thought. The stories and teachings from centuries ago still hold a timeless relevance, each narrative a reflection of life's enduring truths.

The story of Ruth captures my attention with its themes of loyalty and change. Her life, marked by significant loss, mirrors the difficult choices I've faced. Ruth's commitment to Naomi, choosing an uncertain future over the comfort of her past, speaks to the strength found in embracing change and the value of loyalty.

Solomon's wisdom, too, draws me in. His understanding of life's transitory nature and the pursuit of lasting fulfillment echoes in my own experiences. The futility of seeking momentary pleasures and the richness found in wisdom and understanding resonate with my journey. His proverbs, full of insights about human behavior and the essence of a meaningful life, seem written for every generation, including mine.

As I immerse myself in these stories, I am struck by their

enduring relevance. They are not mere historical accounts, but vibrant lessons on character, faith, and the human spirit. These ancient scriptures provide a lens through which I can view and understand my own life - a bridge connecting my present with a distant, yet ever-relevant past.

The ancient pages of the Bible lay open on my lap, their time-worn words offering a treasure trove of wisdom. Today, I am drawn to the deep lessons these biblical stories offer, finding guidance for the modern challenges I face.

In the narratives of David, I see a reflection of our own struggles with inner conflicts and external pressures. David's journey from shepherd boy to king wasn't just a tale of ascension but a story of moral complexities and personal growth. His battles, both on the fields and within his soul, remind me of our own battles in a world that is often confusing and challenging. From David, I learn the importance of courage and integrity, even when faced with daunting challenges.

Then, there's Esther, a beacon of bravery and strategic wisdom. In her story, I find a powerful example of how one can navigate the complexities of life with grace and courage. Her ability to stand up for her people, risking her own safety, teaches me about the strength of conviction and the power of taking calculated risks for the greater good.

Joseph's saga, laden with betrayal and forgiveness, speaks directly to the heart of human relationships. His journey from being sold into slavery by his own brothers to rising as a leader in Egypt teaches me about the power of forgiveness. His ability to forgive those who wronged him and see the larger picture of his life's purpose is a lesson in overcoming bitterness and finding meaning in our trials.

The wisdom of Solomon, renowned for his discernment, also holds valuable lessons. His understanding of human nature and his quest for true wisdom over superficial gains is a stark reminder of the importance of seeking depth and substance in our lives. In a world often captivated by the allure of material success, Solomon's wisdom is a guiding light towards a path of true fulfillment and enlightenment.

Reflecting on the parables of Jesus, I find timeless insights into human behavior and morality. These simple stories are a reminder of the values of compassion, humility, and love. In a world where we are often divided by differences, these teachings call us to look beyond the superficial and connect with the essence of our shared humanity.

As I ponder these stories, I am struck by their enduring relevance. They are not just historical accounts; they are vibrant lessons on character, faith, and the human spirit. They offer a lens through which we can view and understand our own lives—a bridge connecting our present with a distant, yet ever-relevant past.

In these ancient scriptures, I find not just guidance but also comfort. They remind me that, though times have changed, the core of human experience remains constant. The challenges, emotions, and decisions we face today are not so different from those encountered by these biblical figures.

So, as I continue on my journey, I carry with me the wisdom of these stories. They remind me to face life's challenges with courage and integrity, to stand up for what is right, to forgive and find meaning in my trials, to seek true wisdom and depth, and to embrace compassion and love in my interactions.

These ancient lessons, gleaned from the scriptures, are more than just historical narratives; they are a guiding light for navigating the complexities of our modern world. And in them, I find the strength and wisdom to face each day with hope and conviction.

As I settle into the quiet of my study, the world's subtle noises fading into the background, I'm deeply moved by the realization that the challenges and triumphs of the past aren't just historical footnotes; they closely mirror our own modern struggles and victories. The Bible's ancient narratives, from the saga of Moses to the journey of the Israelites, reflect the universal themes of freedom, oppression, and the quest for a promised land, deeply paralleling today's struggles for human rights and social justice.

The story of Moses, a seminal figure in the Exodus, speaks volumes about the fight against subjugation and the yearning for freedom. This narrative, so central to Jewish history, echoes in the modern context as a symbol of resistance against oppression and the unyielding desire for a better, more just society. It's a reminder of our ongoing fight against societal injustices and the enduring human spirit that seeks to create a fairer world.

In the accounts of the Judges, like Deborah and Gideon, I find parallels in their leadership during times of crisis. Their stories of rising to the occasion, guiding their people through tumultuous times, and making tough decisions resonate with our contemporary leaders' challenges in navigating complex political and social landscapes.

The life of King David, from his humble beginnings as a shepherd to his ascent as a monarch, mirrors our own journeys of personal growth and leadership. His triumphs and failures, particularly his moral and ethical dilemmas, reflect the complexities we face in our pursuit of success and the importance of maintaining integrity and humility.

The wisdom literature, particularly the book of Proverbs, offers timeless insights into practical living, addressing themes like stewardship, interpersonal relationships, and work ethics, which are highly relevant in our current societal context. The prophets, with their calls for social justice and spiritual renewal, speak to our modern challenges. Figures like Isaiah and Jeremiah, with their passionate advocacy for societal reform and faithfulness to God's principles, remind us of the need for ethical leadership and social responsibility in our times.

As I reflect on these stories, I'm inspired by their depth and relevance. They aren't just tales from a distant past; they are lessons for living a principled and fulfilling life today. Their themes of freedom, leadership, moral integrity, and social justice continue to guide and inspire us in navigating the complexities of our contemporary world. The scriptures of the Bible are more than ancient texts, they are a manual for life, offering timeless wisdom that empowers us to take control of our own destinies.

The stories of biblical figures are not mere narratives; they are life lessons in courage, faith, and transformation. Consider Joseph, who, despite being betrayed and sold into slavery, rose to prominence by trusting in God and harnessing his innate abilities. His story teaches us about the power of forgiveness and the strength to overcome adversity.

Then, there's the wisdom of Solomon, who sought understanding above all else. His quest for knowledge and discernment is a call for us to value wisdom and apply it in our daily lives. Solomon's reign, marked by peace and prosperity, illustrates how wisdom can lead to positive outcomes in our own lives.

The Psalms offer a treasure of emotional honesty and spiritual depth. David's candid expressions of fear, joy, sorrow, and hope are a reminder that embracing our emotions and laying them before God is a path to healing and strength.

Jesus' teachings, parables, and life are the epitome of love, sacrifice, and leadership. His emphasis on love and compassion, forgiveness, and serving others outlines a blueprint for a life filled with purpose and fulfillment. He exemplifies how to navigate life's challenges with grace and to impact the world positively.

The Bible also addresses the struggles of everyday life – financial stewardship, interpersonal relationships, work ethics, and finding peace amidst chaos. Proverbs, for instance, offer practical guidance on prudent living, while the Epistles provide insights into leading a life that honors God and benefits others.

The Bible is not just a historical document; it's a living guide that speaks into our modern lives. It encourages us to take the reins of our existence, to live with purpose and intention. By applying its teachings, we can navigate life's complexities with wisdom, find solace in times of distress, and build a legacy that resonates with love, integrity, and kindness.

As we close this chapter, I invite you to open your heart to the timeless lessons of the Bible. Let its teachings mold your character, guide your decisions, and illuminate your path. In its pages, find the courage to shape your life story, to be the architect of your destiny, and to live a life that echoes the wisdom of the ages.

Chapter 8: Unveiling Dignity

Discovering My True Purpose — My Journey

In the pursuit of self-awareness and purpose, each of us embarks on a unique journey. This chapter is a reflection, a guide, on how one might navigate the paths of self-discovery and purpose realization. It begins with a resonating thought: "The longest journey is the journey inward," as once mused by Dag Hammarskjöld. This chapter aims to be a companion in that journey, offering insights and experiences that mirror the universal quest for understanding one's true purpose and self-worth.

The journey to self-discovery often starts with questions that challenge our core beliefs. In the early stages, it's common to feel adrift, unsure of one's place in the world. This phase is characterized by introspection, questioning, and often, a sense of restlessness. The key here is to embrace this quest for knowledge, to be open to exploring the depths of one's soul.

As the journey progresses, one encounters various experiences that shape and redefine their understanding of self. These might include educational pursuits, travel, meaningful relationships, and even periods of solitude. Each experience serves as a catalyst for growth, pushing one towards a deeper understanding of their values, passions, and aspirations.

There often comes a turning point – a moment of clarity where one's purpose begins to crystallize. This might be triggered by a significant event, a realization, or a simple moment of joy. It's a time when one begins to understand their unique strengths and how they can contribute to the world in a meaningful way.

An essential step in this journey is realizing and accepting one's self-worth. This involves acknowledging personal achievements, embracing individuality, and understanding that self worth is not determined by external validation but by one's own sense of inner value and contribution.

Finally, the journey leads to a life lived with purpose. This doesn't necessarily mean grandiose achievements but living in alignment with one's values and using one's strengths to contribute positively to the world. It could be through one's profession, volunteering, creative pursuits, or simply by being a kind and understanding person in daily interactions.

The journey to understanding and realizing one's purpose and self-worth is ongoing. It evolves as one grows and experiences life. The key takeaway is to remain open, curious, and accepting of oneself, understanding that this journey is not just about finding a destination but about growing and evolving every step of the way.

This section delves into the initial spark that ignites the journey of self-discovery. Often, it begins with a moment, an experience, or a thought that shifts one's perspective. It could be as simple as reading a book that opens new horizons, a conversation that challenges long-held beliefs, or an event that disrupts the comfortable patterns of daily life. This spark is crucial as it awakens a deeper curiosity about oneself and one's place in the world.

To illustrate this, consider the story of my friend Kieran, a young professional who seemed to have it all - a successful career, a busy social life, and all the trappings of success. However, he felt a persistent sense of emptiness, a nagging feeling that something vital was missing. The turning point came unexpectedly during a solo trip to a remote village. Away from the hustle and bustle of city life, Kieran found a peace and clarity that had been elusive. This experience sparked a reevaluation of priorities and values, leading Kieran on a path of self-discovery and transformation.

Like him, many of us encounter moments that propel us into questioning and exploring our inner world. These moments are the seeds of self-discovery, opening doors to a journey that can be as challenging as it is rewarding.
Now, we will explore the importance of reflective exercises that help us ponder past experiences and understand their impact on our lives. Reflecting on one's life journey can reveal deep insights about personal values, aspirations, and purpose.

An effective reflective exercise is to journal about life events, particularly focusing on those moments that sparked a change in perspective or a deeper understanding of oneself. By writing these experiences down and examining them, patterns and significant life lessons often emerge. This process can be incredibly revealing, providing clarity and direction.

To illustrate this, I'll share a personal story. My journey of self-discovery led me to a sense of peace and purpose through my faith, particularly in the teachings of the Old Testament. Growing up in a secular environment, I had always felt a sense of spiritual emptiness, a gap in my understanding of the world and my place in it. It was during a challenging phase in life, filled with uncertainty and introspection, that I found solace in religious texts. The stories and teachings of the Old Testament resonated deeply with me, providing a sense of comfort and clarity I had never experienced before.

This encounter with faith was a pivotal moment in my life. It offered a new lens through which to view the world and understand my experiences. The wisdom and guidance I found in these ancient texts helped me navigate life with a renewed sense of purpose and conviction. It was a transformative realization that reshaped not only my personal beliefs but also my approach to life and my interactions with others.

This personal story is evidence on how reflective practices can lead to realizations and shifts in our life's trajectory. By taking the time to explore and understand our past experiences, we open ourselves up to new insights and pathways, much like my own journey to finding peace in faith.

In the journey of self-discovery, individuals often face a variety of obstacles, including self doubt and societal pressures. Addressing these challenges is a crucial step in truly unveiling and embracing one's true self.

One of the most pervasive challenges is self-doubt. This internal barrier often manifests as a critical inner voice, casting doubt on one's abilities, choices, and worth. Overcoming self-doubt requires a deliberate effort to recognize and challenge these negative thoughts, and to cultivate a more positive and affirming mindset.

Societal pressures also present a significant obstacle. Many cultures and communities have set expectations and norms, and deviating from these can lead to feelings of isolation or fear of judgment. Choosing a path that is authentic to oneself, especially when it contradicts societal expectations, demands bravery and tenacity.

A notable real-life example of overcoming these challenges is the story of J.K. Rowling. Before she became one of the most successful authors in the world, Rowling faced numerous rejections and hardships. As a single mother living on welfare, she struggled with deep self-doubt and societal stigma. Despite these challenges, she persisted in writing the "Harry Potter" series, a project that she believed in passionately. Her perseverance paid off, but it required overcoming significant personal and societal obstacles. Rowling's story exemplifies the courage it takes to follow one's dreams in the face of adversity, and how doing so can lead to extraordinary success and fulfillment.

These examples and insights aim to inspire and encourage those on their own path of self discovery, highlighting that while the journey may be fraught with challenges, overcoming them is both possible and rewarding.
This questionnaire is designed to guide you through a series of introspective questions, helping you to uncover insights about your passions, values, and potential purpose. Take your time with each question and answer as honestly as possible.

1. Passions and Interests
• What activities do you enjoy doing in your free time?
• Can you recall a project or activity that you worked on tirelessly, not because you had to, but because you loved it?
• What topics do you find yourself reading about or researching often?

2. Skills and Talents
• What are three skills that others often compliment you?
• Think of a time you solved a difficult problem. What abilities helped you overcome it?
• Are there tasks or activities that you find easy while others might struggle?

3. Values and Beliefs
• What are five values that are most important to you in life?
• When have you felt most proud of a decision you made? What does this tell you about your values?
• Are there causes or issues that you feel strongly about?

4. Life Experiences
• Reflect on a challenging time in your life. What did it teach you about yourself? • Describe a peak experience in your life – a time when you felt the most alive. What elements made it so special?
• Have there been turning points in your life that changed your perspective or direction?

5. Dreams and Aspirations
• If there were no limits, what would you want to achieve in your life? • Imagine your ideal day ten years from now. What are you doing, and who are you with? • What have you always wanted to do but haven't yet tried? Why?

6. Legacy and Impact
• How do you want to be remembered by your friends and family?
• What kind of impact do you want to have on your community or the world?
• Are there changes you want to see in the world? How can you contribute to making them happen?

After completing this questionnaire, take some time to

reflect on your answers. Look for patterns or recurring themes, as they can be clues to your underlying passions and purpose. Remember, the journey of self-discovery is ongoing, and your answers may evolve over time. Journaling is a powerful method for self-reflection. It involves writing down thoughts, feelings, and experiences, which can lead to valuable insights. Some prompts to start with could be:

- What activities make me lose track of time?
- When have I felt the most fulfilled or happy?
- What are the recurring themes or patterns in my life?
- If money were no object, what would I spend my life doing?
- What are the challenges I've overcome, and what have they taught me?

Meditation or Mindfulness Techniques: These practices are centered around cultivating a heightened state of awareness and presence. Engaging in meditation or mindfulness can help quiet the mind, making it easier to listen to one's inner voice and intuition. This can be particularly effective in reducing the noise of external expectations and pressures, allowing for a clearer understanding of one's personal desires and goals.

Each of these exercises serves a distinct purpose in the journey of self-discovery. The self assessment questionnaires provide a structured approach to understanding oneself, and journaling prompts facilitate deeper emotional and introspective exploration, and meditation or mindfulness techniques offer a way to center oneself and connect with inner wisdom. By engaging in these activities, individuals can take significant steps towards uncovering their purpose and forging a path that aligns with their true self.

Once you've begun to uncover your purpose, the next step

is integrating this newfound understanding into your daily life. This section provides strategies for doing so and shares stories of how embracing one's purpose can lead to a life of dignity and fulfillment.

Begin by setting clear intentions and goals that align with your purpose. These can be short term or long-term goals, but they should be directly connected to the core aspects of what you've identified as your purpose. This could involve career changes, pursuing new hobbies, or dedicating time to causes that matter to you.

Integrate your purpose into your daily routine. If your purpose is related to creativity, dedicate time each day to your art. If it's about helping others, find small ways to contribute to your community regularly. Consistency is key in living out your purpose.

Surround yourself with people who support and understand your purpose. This could mean joining like-minded groups, seeking mentors, or simply sharing your journey with friends and family. A supportive community can provide encouragement and motivation.

Be open to the fact that your understanding of your purpose might evolve over time. Stay flexible and adapt your goals as needed. Life is dynamic, and so is the journey of living out your purpose.

The journey of discovering one's purpose is a continuous, ever-evolving process. Life is dynamic, and as we grow and change, our understanding of our purpose may also shift. This ongoing journey requires patience, perseverance, and an openness to adapt. Regular self reflection is vital in this process, ensuring that we remain aligned with our evolving purpose. Keeping an open mind, exploring new interests, and seeking out challenges are also essential elements. They help us to grow, learn, and deepen our understanding of ourselves and our place in the world.

In this chapter, we have navigated the path of self-discovery and realization of one's purpose and self-worth. We began with the initial spark that ignites the quest for self-aware-ness and delved into the importance of introspection and overcoming obstacles such as self-doubt and societal pres-sures. The practical steps provided, from self-assessment questionnaires to mindfulness practices, are tools to aid in this discovery. The integration of one's purpose into daily life is essential for a fulfilling existence, and the continu-ous nature of this journey underscores the importance of growth and adaptation.

As you turn the page, remember that the journey of self-discovery is a personal and unique adventure. It is a path filled with uncertainties and challenges, but also with immense joy and fulfillment. May the insights and stories shared in this chapter serve as a source of inspiration and guidance on your journey. Embrace this path with an open heart and mind, and let your journey of self-discovery un-fold in its own beautiful and unpredictable way.

Chapter 9: Crazy Faith

Embracing Radical Belief—Current Life and the Future

In a world where certainty is often prized above all, the concept of "Crazy Faith" emerges as astriking and daring philosophy. This chapter delves into defining what exactly constitutesCrazy Faith and explores its critical role in fostering personal growth and transformation.

At its core, Crazy Faith is about embracing a level of belief in oneself and one's future that goes beyond the conventional. It's a mindset that challenges the norms, defies the odds, and transcends the usual expectations of what is possible. This type of faith is characterized by an audacious confidence, a conviction in the face of uncertainty, and a relentless pursuit of one's goals despite the apparent obstacles.

The importance of such a radical belief system in personal development cannot be understated. It serves as a powerful catalyst for change, pushing individuals to break free from the shackles of doubt and fear that often inhibit growth. Embracing Crazy Faith means allowing oneself to dream big, set ambitious goals, and passionately chase after them, regardless of the skepticism or disbelief of others.

This chapter will illustrate how adopting a mindset of Crazy Faith can lead to remarkable transformations. It's about understanding that the journey towards realizing one's potential is often marked by leaps of faith that seem irrational or ungrounded to the outside world. Yet, it is precisely this kind of faith that fuels innovation, drives breakthroughs, and leads to extraordinary achievements.

Crazy Faith is about daring to believe in the incredible, the uncharted, and the seemingly impossible. It's about finding strength in one's convictions and using that strength to propel oneself forward. As we explore this concept, we will uncover how Crazy Faith can be a transformative force in both personal and professional spheres, leading to unparalleled growth and fulfillment.

Understanding Crazy Faithrequires redefining what 'crazy' means in this context. Here, 'crazy' is not about irrationality or mental instability; instead, it denotes something extraordinary, unconventional, and fearless. It's a perspective that challenges standard norms and embraces the audacity of believing in something beyond the ordinary. This chapter explores the depths of Crazy Faith, examining its psychological and emotional dimensions and how it stands distinct from mere blind optimism or recklessness.

In the realm of Crazy Faith, 'crazy' symbolizes the courage to step beyond traditional boundaries. It's about embracing ideas and ambitions that others might dismiss as unrealistic or overly ambitious. This kind of faith is not restricted by common perceptions of what is achievable; instead, it thrives on unique, bold visions. It's a fearless approach to life, marked by a willingness to pursue extraordinary paths that might seem daunting or uncharted to others.

Embracing Crazy Faith is as much a psychological journey as it is an emotional one. Psychologically, it requires a paradigm shift—a move away from conventional thinking patterns towards a mindset that is open to vast possibilities. Emotionally, it demands a strong inner conviction and an belief in yourself. This chapter delves into the mental fortitude required to maintain this faith, especially in the face of skepticism or adversity. It also explores the emotional journey of holding onto one's beliefs, the exhilaration of chasing ambitious dreams, and the inner peace that comes from aligning with one's true aspirations.

While Crazy Faith is about bold belief and daring steps, it is crucial to differentiate it from blind optimism or recklessness. Blind optimism is hoping for the best without acknowledging the realities and challenges that might arise. Recklessness, on the other hand, involves taking risks without considering the consequences. "Crazy Faith," however, is a more nuanced and strategic approach. It involves a conscious acknowledgment of risks and challenges but choosing to believe and act anyway. This chapter will explore how to balance audacious faith with practical wisdom, ensuring that one's journey towards extraordinary goals is both bold and mindful.

Now, we will delve into the historical and cultural dimensions of "Crazy Faith," highlighting examples from various epochs and societies. These instances demonstrate not only the timeless and universal nature of such faith but also its significant impact on both societal and personal transformations.

Throughout history, there have been numerous figures and movements that exemplified Crazy Faith. These range from visionary leaders and innovators to entire cultural movements that dared to challenge the status quo. For instance, consider the scientific pioneers who proposed theories that defied the accepted knowledge of their times, or the social reformers who believed in the possibility of a better world against all odds. Such individuals and groups often faced skepticism and opposition, yet their unwavering faith in their visions led to groundbreaking discoveries and societal shifts.

In various cultures, Crazy Faith has manifested in different forms. It might appear as the unshakeable spirit of a small community fighting for its rights or the ambitious dreams of artists and thinkers in societies that stifled creative expression. Each of these examples reveals how a deep, almost radical belief in a cause or an idea can lead to significant advancements and cultural enrichment.

The impact of Crazy Faith is two-fold: societal and personal. On a societal level, such faith has often been the driving force behind major changes and advancements. It has led to revolutions, renaissances, and reforms that have reshaped civilizations. These changes reflect the power of collective belief and action driven by a shared vision that transcends conventional limits.

On a personal level, Crazy Faith can be a transformative force in your life. It can lead to personal breakthroughs, allowing you to reach heights they never thought possible. By exploring these historical and cultural examples, we can see how embracing Crazy Faith has enabled people to overcome seemingly insurmountable obstacles, achieve remarkable feats, and alter the course of their lives.

If we view Crazy Faith through the lens of personal narratives, it brings to light inspiring real-life stories of individuals from various walks of life who exemplified the essence of taking bold steps of faith. Each story not only highlights the challenges these individuals faced but also demonstrates how their faith led to positive, life-altering outcomes.

You might read about a young inventor who, against all advice, pursued an idea that everyone dismissed, leading to a revolutionary invention. Another story might tell of someone who, despite facing severe personal challenges, held onto their belief and achieved their lifelong dream against all odds. Each story is unique, yet they all share a common thread – the extraordinary impact of holding onto faith in one's abilities and aspirations.

Take for example, Elon Musk - His journey with SpaceX exemplifies "Crazy Faith." When Musk started the company, the idea of a private enterprise in space exploration was nearly unthinkable. He faced technical failures and widespread skepticism. Yet, his steadfast belief in his vision led SpaceX to make historic achievements, including the first privately-funded spacecraft to reach the International Space Station. Musk risked personal bankruptcy, investing his own funds into SpaceX while facing technical setbacks and public doubt.

Furthermore, the story of how JK Rowling wrote and published the Harry Potter series is a classic example of Crazy Faith. Facing personal hardships, including financial struggles as a single mother, Rowling persisted with her writing. Despite numerous rejections from publishers, her belief in her story's potential eventually led to the creation of one of the most successful book series in history. Rowling coped with personal and financial struggles, persevering through the rejection of her manuscript by multiple publishers.

Steve Jobs' journey with Apple is another demonstration to Crazy Faith. After being ousted from the company he co-founded, he returned years later to save it from near bankruptcy. His unshakable belief in his vision for Apple and its products, like the iPhone, transformed not only the company but the entire tech industry. Jobs navigated through professional setbacks and the challenge of reinventing a company on the brink of failure.

Their Crazy Faith manifested not only in persistence but also in innovation, creativity, and the ability to inspire others. The outcomes of their journeys were not just personal successes but also wide-reaching impacts on society and their respective industries.

These stories show that Crazy Faith is about more than just achieving goals; it's about transforming visions into reality, often changing the world in the process. They serve as powerful examples of how belief in oneself and one's ideas, against all odds, can lead to truly remarkable life journeys.

These personal accounts are not just about success; they also candidly discuss the hurdles and setbacks encountered along the way. The challenges featured in these stories are as varied as the individuals themselves, ranging from financial struggles, societal pushback, personal doubts, to external naysayers. These stories provide an honest look at the reality of pursuing a path fueled by Crazy Faith.

What makes these stories truly gripping is how each of their faith became the key to overcoming these challenges. Whether it was finding innovative solutions to problems, garnering support from unexpected sources, or simply the inner strength to persevere – their Crazy Faith acted as a guiding light. The outcomes of these journeys are not just achievements or successes in the conventional sense, but personal growth and fulfillment.

Now that we have discussed Crazy Faith, it's about making this concept a tangible part of your everyday actions and thoughts. Here, we'll discuss exercises and strategies to help cultivate a strong belief in yourself and your dreams, making Crazy Faith an active element of your life.

Guidance on How to Practice and Incorporate Crazy Faith in Daily Life:

• Begin by establishing goals that stretch beyond your current comfort zone. These goals should be ambitious but achievable, challenging you to extend your limits. Choose objectives that both excite and slightly intimidate you.

• Regularly practice visualization. Dedicate time each day to vividly imagine achieving your goals. Envision the success in great detail – the feelings, the surroundings, the sounds, and how others react. This practice helps solidify the belief in your dream's feasibility.

• Use daily affirmations to reinforce belief in your abilities and goals. Positive self-talk is crucial for shifting your mindset from doubt to confidence, a key component of maintaining Crazy Faith.

• Find role models who embody Crazy Faith. Learn from their paths, understand their mindset, and draw inspiration from their stories. Their journeys can serve as both motivation and a guide for developing similar faith in your life.

Practical Exercises and Strategies to Cultivate a Strong Belief in Yourself and YourDreams:

• Keep a journal to reflect on your progress, confront your fears, and document the steps you're taking toward your goals. This practice helps maintain clarity of purpose and track your development.

• Surround yourself with people who support and believe in your vision. A network of encouragers can provide the necessary motivation and feedback to stay grounded and focused.

• Begin taking small, calculated risks that align with your goals. This builds confidence and helps you become comfortable with stepping out of your comfort zone.

• Commit to ongoing learning and remain open to adjusting your approach. Being adaptable is crucial when navigating the unpredictable journey toward your dreams.

• Engage in mindfulness and stress management practices. Keeping your mind clear and managing stress is essential for sustaining the mental energy needed for Crazy Faith.

Incorporating these practices into your daily life helps you embody the principles of Crazy Faith. It's about fostering a mindset that constantly propels you toward your dreams, bolstered by the belief that your aspirations are not only achievable but within your grasp.

One of the most common fears you may have is the apprehension of failure. It's essential to recognize that failure is a natural part of the journey towards success. Reframing failure as a learning opportunity rather than a setback can significantly diminish its intimidating effect.

Doubting your own capabilities is a major obstacle. To combat this, focus on past successes and achievements, no matter how small. Reminding yourself of these victories can boost confidence and mitigate self-doubt.

Furthermore, concern about what others think can be paralyzing. It's important to remember that the pursuit of your dreams should be for personal fulfillment and not to meet others' expectations. Cultivating a mindset that prioritizes personal satisfaction over external approval is key.

The unknown aspects of pursuing big dreams can be daunting. Accepting that uncertainty is a part of the process and focusing on what can be controlled – like effort and attitude – helps in maintaining a positive outlook.

Techniques for Maintaining Faith During Challenging Times:

• Practices like mindfulness and meditation can be effective in managing stress and anxiety. They help in staying present and focused, preventing being overwhelmed by future uncertainties or past regrets.

• Regularly using positive affirmations and visualization techniques can reinforce faith and belief in one's goals. Visualizing successful outcomes helps in creating a mental image of achieving one's dreams, bolstering confidence and determination.

• Leaning on a supportive network of friends, family, or mentors can provide encouragement and advice. Sometimes, just talking about doubts and fears with someone understanding can offer new perspectives and solutions.

• Being open to adapt and adjust plans as needed can alleviate the pressure of having to follow a rigid path. Flexibility allows for navigating obstacles more effectively andreduces the stress of unforeseen challenges.

• Acknowledging and celebrating small accomplishments along the journey can help in maintaining motivation and faith. It serves as a reminder of the progress being made, even when the end goal seems far away.

Creating and nurturing an environment conducive to Crazy Faith not only bolsters individual efforts but also contributes significantly to sustaining radical belief. It involves cultivating a supportive community and recognizing the pivotal role of mentors, friends, and family in this journey.

Surround yourself with individuals who share similar values of boldness and ambition. This network can be built through joining groups, attending events, or participating in forums that align with your goals. A community of like-minded individuals provides a space for sharing ideas, offering encouragement, and receiving constructive feedback.

Engage with environments that inspire and motivate you. This could be physical spaces like co-working hubs or creative studios, or virtual spaces such as online communities and forums. Being in an environment that stimulates creativity and ambition can significantly boost your Crazy Faith.

Actively contribute to creating an atmosphere where positivity is nurtured. This can be done by celebrating others' successes, offering encouragement during setbacks, and maintaining an overall optimistic outlook.

Mentors also play a crucial role in guiding and shaping your journey. They can provide valuable insights, advice, and guidance based on their experience. A mentor who understands and supports your Crazy Faith can help navigate challenges and keep you aligned with your goals.
Friends can offer emotional support, understanding, and camaraderie. Building friendships with individuals who respect and believe in your vision can create a strong support system. They can be sounding boards for your ideas and reliable sources of encouragement.

Family members can be foundational in instilling and nurturing belief in oneself. Their support can come in various forms – from providing encouragement, to offering practical help, to simply believing in your potential. Open communication about your aspirations and challenges with family can foster a supportive home environment.

By cultivating such an environment and nurturing these relationships, you create a fertile ground for Crazy Faith to thrive. This supportive backdrop not only reinforces your belief in your own potential but also surrounds you with the energy and inspiration necessary to pursue your dreams with conviction.

As you close this chapter on Crazy Faith, it's time to take that vital first step towards a radical belief in yourself and your future. This isn't just about reading and understanding; it's about doing and transforming. Let's begin with some introspection to gauge your current level of Crazy Faith and then move towards creating a personal action plan to cultivate it further.

Start by asking yourself some key questions:

• What are your deepest beliefs about your abilities and potential? Do you find yourselfconstrained by what you or others perceive as possible?

• Reflect on your past decisions where you might have shown elements of 'Crazy Faith'. What were those moments, and what were the outcomes?

• Consider the fears and doubts that typically hold you back. How do you usually confront these feelings?

• Try to visualize achieving your biggest dreams. How clear and detailed are these visions in your mind?

• Think about your comfort level with taking risks. Do you shy away from uncertainty, or do you find excitement in it?

Now, let's build your personal action plan to start practicing "Crazy Faith":

• Set yourself bold and inspiring goals. These should be goals that excite you and push
your boundaries.

• Break down these goals into smaller, actionable steps. Create a roadmap that leads you to your larger vision.

• Identify people who can support you on this journey. This could be mentors, friends, family, or even peers who share your aspirations.

• Commit to learning continuously. Whether it's reading, taking courses, or engaging in new experiences, make sure you're always adding to your skillset and knowledge.

• Establish a routine for regular reflection. Use this time to assess your progress, makenecessary adjustments, and renew your commitment to your goals.

• Don't forget to manage stress. Incorporate practices like meditation, exercise, or engaging in hobbies to maintain a clear and focused mind.

Remember, Crazy Faith is more than just a concept; it's a lifestyle. It's about believing in the extraordinary within you and taking concrete steps towards making your dreams a reality. So,take a deep breath, believe in yourself, and embark on this exciting journey. The path ahead is yours to shape.

SECTION II: RISING FROM ADVERSITY

Chapter 10: Discomfort

From the Pit to the Palace — Transforming Tragedy into Triumph

"But as for you, you meant evil against me; but God meant it for good, in order to bring it about as it is this day, to save many people alive."

The journey I have chronicled in the previous pages is not just my story, but a testimony to the strength that lies within each of us. Reflecting on the past chapters, it's clear that the path I've walked was not just about facing adversity; it was about transforming it. From the early days of confusion and struggle, through the turbulent times of loss and uncertainty, each step was a lesson in fortitude.

Now, as I stand at this pivotal chapter in my life, I am ready to share how the pain, once a foe, has become an unexpected ally. This is not just about enduring hardship but about reshaping it into a force that propels us forward. In these pages, I will unveil how the darkest moments of my life didn't just test me; they forged me into who I am today.

As we jump on this chapter, remember: our greatest challenges are not the end of our story; they are the crucibles in which our true strength is forged. This is the story of how I learned to turn my pain into a powerful motivator, a beacon that guided me through the darkness towards a future I once thought impossible.

In my journey, pain has been an ever-present companion, taking various forms and shapes. It has manifested as emotional aches, physical discomfort, and psychological distress. Each type, unique in its impact, has shaped the course of my life in profound ways.

Emotional pain, for me, was like a silent tide, ebbing and flowing with the circumstances of life. It came in the form of heartaches from lost love, the grief of losing close ones, and the sting of betrayal. These experiences, while deeply scarring, also offered insights into the depth of human emotions and the strength it takes to heal.

Physical pain was more straightforward, yet equally challenging. The wear and tear on my body from years of pushing its limits taught me about endurance and the importance of listening to the signals my body sends. Whether it was recovering from an injury or dealing with chronic conditions, physical pain brought an awareness of the fragility and resilience of the human body.

Psychological pain, perhaps the most complex, was a labyrinth of thoughts and feelings. Struggling with anxiety and moments of depression, I learned how mental pain can skew perception and cloud judgment. It showed me the importance of mental health and the need for self-care and support.

Throughout my life, I encountered individuals with stories of pain that mirrored and differed from my own. A friend who battled severe depression taught me about the silent struggles that often go unnoticed. A young athlete I mentored, dealing with a career-ending injury, showed me the heartache that comes with lost dreams and the courage it takes to forge new ones.

Pain, in all its forms, influences our thoughts, feelings, and behaviors in ways we often don't realize. It can be a weight dragging us down or a force pushing us to grow and change. As we delve deeper into this chapter, I will share more about how these different shades of pain have
not only affected me but also shaped the person I have become.

In the ancient practice of alchemy, practitioners sought to transform base metals into precious ones, most famously attempting to create gold. This process, often shrouded in mystery and metaphor, serves as a powerful analogy for my own experiences with pain. Just as alchemists labored to transmute lead into gold, I too have worked to transform my deepest pains into invaluable strengths.

This transformation did not happen overnight, nor was it a straightforward process. It began with acceptance – acknowledging the pain rather than fleeing from it. I learned to sit with my discomfort, to understand its roots and triggers. This was not a journey I undertook alone; it involved seeking help, engaging in introspective practices, and sometimes, simply allowing time to work its healing magic.

Turning pain into strength meant reinterpreting my experiences. Where there was once a narrative of victimhood, I gradually wove a story of survival and resilience. I discovered that within the crucible of suffering, lay the seeds of empathy, wisdom, and a deeper appreciation for life. My struggles with loss taught me about the impermanence of life, making me more present and grateful for each moment. Battling physical ailments revealed my body's remarkable capacity for healing and adaptation, leading me to embrace healthier habits and a more balanced lifestyle.

Adversity became a catalyst for self-discovery. In facing my fears and insecurities, I uncovered strengths I never knew I had. I found courage in vulnerability, strength in admitting my limitations, and a sense of purpose in overcoming obstacles. This journey was not about eradicating pain but learning to coexist with it, allowing it to shape me without defining me.

But it was not just my efforts alone that led to this transformation. In the midst of my pain, God broke my way of thinking about myself and how I perceived my life based on my past experiences. He shed a new perspective by creating in me a new heart and a right spirit, breaking my concubine mentality.

In the depths of my pain, I found solace and strength in my faith. It was during these moments of vulnerability that I turned to God, seeking guidance and understanding. In His infinite wisdom, He saw beyond my pain and brokenness, offering a new perspective that shattered the limitations of my past experiences.

As I surrendered to God's will, He worked within me, molding my heart and spirit. He gently chiseled away the walls I had built to protect myself, allowing His light to penetrate the darkest corners of my being. In that sacred space, He rewrote the narrative of my life, erasing the self-doubt and insecurities that had held me captive for so long.

God's transformative power was not limited to surface-level changes; it went deep into the core of my being. He confronted the distorted beliefs I had about myself, challenging the negative self-talk and replacing it with His truth. Through His word and the whispers of His Spirit, He revealed my inherent worth and restored my sense of identity.

One of the most profound ways God worked within me was by breaking the chains of my concubine mentality. This mentality had kept me bound to a cycle of destructive patterns, where I settled for less than what I deserved and believed that I was unworthy of true love and respect. But God, in His mercy and love, shattered those chains and set me free.

With each revelation, God created a new heart within me, one that beat with strength, resilience, and unwavering faith. He infused me with a right spirit, aligning my thoughts and desires with His divine purpose for my life. Through His transformative touch, I found the courage to step into my true identity and embrace the abundant life He had prepared for me.

It is important to note that the transformative work of God does not eliminate pain; rather, it provides a perspective that transcends the pain. In the midst of my struggles, I discovered that God's presence and love were constant, even in the darkest moments. He became my anchor, my source of hope, and my guide through the storms of life.

As I continue to navigate the complexities of pain and its transformation, I hold onto the knowledge that I am not alone. God walks beside me, His hand extended, ready to lead me forward. With His help, I can face the challenges ahead with unwavering faith, knowing that He will use even the most painful experiences to shape me into the person He created me to be.

As we explore further in this chapter, I will share more about how these hard-earned insights have not only transformed my perception of pain but also reshaped my approach to life's challenges.

Transforming pain into a source of motivation and strength is not just a philosophical concept; it requires practical strategies and actionable steps. Over the years, I have developed and employed various techniques to channel my pain into positive outcomes. Here, I share some of these strategies, hoping they might serve as a beacon for others navigating their own tumultuous seas.

The first step in transformation is to acknowledge and accept your pain. Avoiding or suppressing it only gives it more power. I learned to sit with my pain, understand its origins, and respect it as a part of my journey. This recognition was the first step towards using it constructively.

Staying positive in the face of adversity is challenging but crucial. I am aware that it is easier said than done, however, I found solace in daily affirmations, a gratitude journal, and surrounding myself with uplifting influences. When the clouds of pessimism loomed, I reminded myself of past triumphs over difficulties, using them as evidence of my ability to overcome current challenges.

Pain can be a powerful motivator for setting and achieving goals. I used my struggles as a catalyst to pursue ambitions I had previously thought unattainable. This involved breaking down larger goals into smaller, manageable tasks, celebrating small victories, and constantly reassessing and adjusting my approaches based on what I learned from each setback.

Transformation is rarely a solitary journey. Seeking support from friends, family, or professionals can provide new perspectives and coping mechanisms. Additionally, sharing my story with others, and hearing theirs, created a sense of community and mutual growth.

Developing resilience is key to turning pain into strength. This meant learning to adapt to changing circumstances, bouncing back from setbacks, and viewing failures as opportunities for growth. I focused on building emotional resilience through mindfulness, meditation, and
sometimes, simply giving myself permission to feel and heal.

Channeling pain into creative pursuits was another transformative strategy. Whether it was writing, painting, or music, creative expression provided an outlet for my emotions and a way to process and understand my experiences.

In the realm of real-life heroes, there are countless individuals who have successfully transformed their pain into triumph. While it's easy to focus on well-known figures like actors or musicians or models, I find the stories of ordinary people who sought for the betterment of the world equally inspiring.

One such individual is Nelson Mandela. Born in apartheid-era South Africa, Mandela faced immense racial discrimination and oppression. He dedicated his life to fighting against racial injustice and inequality. Despite being imprisoned for 27 years, Mandela's determination to end apartheid and promote reconciliation never wavered.

After his release, Mandela became the first black president of South Africa and played a pivotal role in the country's transition to democracy. His story exemplifies the incredible power of perseverance and the impact one person can have on a nation's history.

Another real-life hero is Temple Grandin, an autistic woman who faced numerous challenges in a world that often misunderstood her condition. Temple used her unique perspective to become a prominent animal scientist and advocate for the humane treatment of livestock. Her determination and innovative thinking revolutionized the livestock industry and improved the lives of countless animals.

These stories of individuals demonstrate that triumph over adversity is not limited to the famous and well-known. Ordinary people can achieve extraordinary feats when they possess the determination and resilience to overcome life's challenges. Their stories serve as powerful reminders that, regardless of our circumstances, we all have the potential to turn our pain into triumph and make a positive impact on the world.

With all this being stated, take a moment to pause and understand. What follows is a simple questionnaire, that can help you evaluate your life and reflect on the person you are. As a follow-up exercise, you may re-answer these questions as the person you hope to become and compare the answers.

1. **Self-Reflection:** Recall a challenging situation or adversity you've faced in your life. How did it make you feel, and how did you initially respond?

2. **Personal Strengths:** Identify your own strengths that have helped you overcome adversity. Are there specific qualities or skills you possess that have played a role in your success?

3. **Triumph Over Adversity:** Reflect on a specific instance when you overcame a significant challenge. What contributed to your success, and what did you learn from that experience?

4. Role Models: Who are some individuals you admire for their ability to overcome difficulties? What specific qualities or actions of these individuals inspire you, and how can you apply them to your life?

5. Goals and Determination: Think about a personal goal or dream you are pursuing. How has your determination influenced your progress, and what steps can you take to stay committed to achieving it?

6. Empowerment: Consider moments when you felt empowered after overcoming obstacles. How did this sense of empowerment affect your self-confidence, and how can you harness it in other areas of your life?

7. Support Network: Reflect on the people in your life who have supported you during tough times. How have these relationships impacted your ability to persevere, and how can you strengthen your support network?

8. Adversity as Growth: Recall an experience where adversity led to personal growth or positive change. What lessons did you learn from that situation, and how did it shape your character?

9. Action Plan: Identify a current challenge or obstacle you're facing. Create a plan outlining the steps you can take to address it. Consider the role of determination in executing this plan.

10. Inspiration: Seek out stories of individuals who have triumphed over adversity. Explore books, documentaries, or interviews about their journeys. Reflect on how their stories relate to your own life and aspirations.

These reflection questions and exercises are intended to help you explore your personal experiences, strengths, and areas for growth in the context of overcoming challenges. By engaging in thoughtful reflection and applying the lessons from this chapter, you can further develop your ability to overcome adversity and achieve your goals.